The Virtual Studio

The Virtual Studio

Moshe Moshkovitz

Focal Press

Boston   Oxford   Auckland   Johannesburg   Melbourne   New Delhi

At the time of going to press, the Israeli company ORAD announced that they had acquired Accom of California. According to a spokesperson for ORAD, the Accom products will continue to be manufactured and will probably be available under the ORAD name. This acquisition now positions ORAD as the leading Virtual Studio Company.

Table of Contents

Preface

The virtual studio is relatively a very young subject in the field of broadcast television. Technical and artistic techniques are involved. I believe that this new technology will shape television as we know it, more than any other. This is why I chose it as the subject of this book.

The virtual studio technology employs the latest in computer hardware and software. The way it works is revolutionary on one hand but it is integrated with the existing conventional TV studio space and equipment and works as part of it.

Traditional studio techniques such as keying are combined with the latest of computer-generated images and animation.

The virtual studio will no doubt change the "look" of many TV programs in the years to come and the look of television in general. It will give it a more modern and "computer age" appearance or any other appearance designers will give it. New possibilities will be opened up in terms of shape, color, texture and movement.

Studio scenery will no longer be limited to what you can build out of the existing materials such as wood, cardboard and metal and to textures you can obtain by using a few cans of paint.

Virtual scenery elements will be able to move in three-dimensional space, not attached or constrained in any way.

Only the talent and imagination of the designers will limit the appearance and the diversity of virtual scenery. The traditional way in which TV programs are produced today will be changed.

More graphical designers and computer operators and engineers will probably be employed by studios, and less scenery builders and stagehands.

The contribution of the virtual studio will grow with the improvement of computer technology, in itself a fast going process. Some ten companies world-wide invest in research and development of virtual studio systems, and new techniques emerge all the time. Large organizations such as the BBC also invest in research on the subject indicating that they believe in the future of virtual studio.

The intention of this book is to set out before the reader the subject of virtual studio at several levels.

This book will explain what this technology is all about. It will give examples of what can be achieved.

For technical people, in addition to the general understanding what the virtual studio is, detailed description of different methods and techniques will be provided. Subjects such as camera movement tracking systems, computer hardware and software involved and installation are included. A detailed comparison table between the different system is provided.

This book will help you decide what is the best way to integrate a virtual studio into an existing facility, and what needs to be purchased in terms of hardware and software. Requirements of the system in terms of space, connections to existing equipment in the facility and manpower will also be provided. Subjects such as graphic design, lighting and chroma-key are discussed in detail. A variety of system configuration drawings are provided.

In this work you will also find information regarding the problems involved in working with virtual studios.

This work should enhance the knowledge of the subject to a degree that will allow asking the right questions and exploring the details when in contact or negotiations with virtual studio manufacturers, suppliers and operators.

The intended audience of this work is a wide spectrum of people in different disciplines: Managerial staff such as station managers and executive producers; technical staff such as technical managers, engineers, technicians, and different kinds of operators in the studio; artistic people such as art directors, graphical designers, set designers, cameramen and lighting designers; students of communications and television studies at different levels; and, of course, all those who want to enrich their knowledge of modern TV technology.

The virtual studio technology cannot be ignored. Before deciding whether to use such techniques, a basic understanding of the possibilities and requirements is needed, something that this book can provide.

Acknowledgments

This book was made possible thanks to the cooperation I had from manufacturers of virtual studio and related technology.

I thank the good people from Accom, Michael Bauer who answered all my questions with great dedication, and Andrew Wojdala who helped me clarify things and sent me his enlightening articles.

I would like to thank Dr. Miki Tamir, Avi Sharir, and Tamir Ben-David from ORAD who helped me with a lot of technical and visual material and connections with virtual studio users worldwide; Nitsan Rachman who is a gifted computer graphics expert; Satyam Prem and Sigalit Elazar, the artists; Effi Dilmoni, the engineer; and last but not least Gal Bar-on from ORAD, for all her efforts.

Thanks are due to Rollin Stanford and MaryEllen Hunt from Evans & Sutherland; Jean Francois Miribel from Getris Images; Andrea Thoma from Thoma-Filmtechnik; Michael Wolfe from Radamec; Shalom Nachshon, Alon Carmeli, Rebecca Fadida and Karni Hertz-Maman from RT-Set; Harold Kalmus from FauxReal; Ori j. Braun and Miri Arie from 3DV systems; Rafi Rothenberg from WDR; Marina Escobar from Discreet Logic; Danny Popkin from the BBC; and Avi Ambar, the director.

Special thanks are due to my good friend, talented and skillful graphic designer, Ronald Basford who did the editing, graphic design, and layout of this book. Without his advice and support, this book would not have been published.

1   A Short History

Since the beginning of television, and especially color television, ways of creating a non-real environment for performers in the studio have been investigated and used. The most common method used was luminance key, and later, when color was introduced, chroma-key. These techniques produced quite convincing results, as long as the camera that shot the scene did not move. Until recently, this was a very serious limitation.

Chroma-key, limited as it is, was used in television mainly for news, weather, children's programs, some video clips and special effects. Different attempts were made to connect in parallel two camera zoom lenses in a way that one control will move both zoom mechanisms at the same time and speed. In this arrangement one camera shot an actor and the other one a picture or artwork used as background in the chroma-key combination. Both cameras could do a zoom in or out motion, and the effect was quite convincing and added a new dimension of movement to chroma-key.

In the mid '70s a motorized easel was used at the BBC, electrically linked to a camera pan and tilt head. It had many disadvantages such as limited range and speed of movement, and ability to use still pictures only. This arrangement was called "Scene-Sync" and despite its limitations was used for the making of several award-winning shows.

The history of the virtual studio as such starts in 1993 when two companies in parallel investigated solutions for chroma-key with a computer-generated image in the background that would move synchronously with camera movement. The two companies were IMP and VAP. The SGI Onyx computer equipped with the Reality-2 graphics engine that was released that year made it possible to get reasonable results. The way to measure camera orientation was to install mechanical sensors in pan and tilt heads, one on every axis of movement. Using this method considerable amounts of time were needed to calibrate the system. The computer models showed then were rather simple, but the overall effect was convincing enough to keep the development going.

VAP joined the Mona-Lisa project funded by the EEC. In this project a number of European companies participated in development together with some universities and the BBC. Mona-Lisa used an early version of pattern recognition.

Virtual studio systems were displayed for the first time to broadcasters in the 1994 International Broadcasting Convention (IBC) in Amsterdam. The systems showed at that time were difficult to set up, unreliable, and expensive, but it didn't stop other manufacturers from joining the adventure and trying to improve the technology.

Many people then believed that virtual studio technology was about to revolutionize the way programs are made, within a very short time. The belief was that graphics engines would develop rapidly, something that as it turned out, did not happen. The improvement in high-end computers was not as fast as in personal computers.

In 1995 ORAD introduced a virtual set system named CyberSet that used an improved tracking system based on pattern recognition. Using a dedicated high-end computer and a two-color grid located on the studio wall, the pattern recognition system was able to work out the exact position of the camera.

Another company, RT-Set, introduced a virtual studio system named Larus. RT-Set used know-how in real-time rendering of large graphic files and movement tracking gathered during years of manufacturing flight simulators.

In 1996 SGI introduced a new graphics engine—"Infinite Reality." This new engine enabled several new improvements including dealing with sets that had an increased number of polygons and for the first time, defocus effects. In the same year the Virtual Scenario system, designed by the BBC and sold by Radamec, was introduced. This is a system that uses a standard video image as background, which is moved in a DVE effect in coordination with foreground camera movement. That year ORAD introduced a stand-alone version of their pattern recognition system that could work with any virtual studio system.

In 1997 the SGI Onyx was no longer alone in the virtual studio arena. Accom introduced their Elset-Live-NT system and Evans & Sutherland introduced the MindSet system, both of which are Windows NT based.

Since then many improvements have been introduced to virtual studio systems and their supporting technologies. Various infrared camera-tracking systems have been introduced by ORAD, Thoma, Hawkeye, Mark Roberts and others. Highly precise sensor pan and tilt heads have been produced by traditional support systems manufacturers such as Radamec and Vinten. Defocused backgrounds providing blur according to the laws of geometric optics are possible. Shadow handling can now enhance realism by casting shadows of real objects on virtual backgrounds. A virtual camera option allows use of a camera located outside the boundaries of the physical studio. Trash-mattes are used to hide parts of the foreground that introduce a problem such as an unlit corner or the studio ceiling. Depth keying systems can map the position of actors in the studio in real time.

These are only some of the innovations introduced during the last few years. Virtual studio systems use highly sophisticated hardware and software, and new features are introduced all the time. At the same time many efforts have been made to allow easier operation and shorter set-up and calibration times.

The history of virtual studio may be only a few years long, but it is full of innovations and award-winnings.

This chapter is partly based on a work written by Danny Popkin from the BBC.

The virtual studio used by the News Department of Israel's Second Television Channel for its Special Millennium Night broadcast (a sample of which can be seen on the CD accompanying this book).

2 What Is a Virtual Studio?

Since the beginning of television, actors in the studio were positioned in front of simple scenery. The function of the scenery together with the appropriate lighting was to create a sense of place, time and atmosphere. The scenery was usually made of wood or cardboard and painted. To a large extent this is the way most scenery is made today.

With the passage of time, it became necessary to offer the viewer extra dimensions and illusions, to break out of the limiting and conventional sets of the early days. The first technique in this direction was keying. During the days of black and white television it was the luminance key, and later on when color TV started, chroma-key was used. The key is a technique whereby certain parts of the background of a picture are replaced by a still picture located in front of a camera in the studio, a prerecorded or live video feed or any other video picture source.

In luminance key luminance levels within the video signal picture information higher or lower than a specific level is taken out, and instead picture information from another "fill" video signal is inserted.

In chroma-key, areas in a picture that have a specific hue and saturation are taken out and replaced by a "fill" picture. The keying technique allows the use of new kinds of backgrounds behind actors in a studio: a weatherperson can appear with a live satellite feed behind him. An actor can appear to be standing outside in the street or in any other open space while actually he is standing in a small studio. In the case of the weatherperson in the studio he is standing in front of a blue background. The satellite feed coming into the studio video mixer replaces the blue parts in the picture that forms his background. The weatherperson will usually see the complete chroma-key effect on a picture monitor in the studio. Most news and weather programs use chroma-key as do children's programs, video clips and every other program where special visual effects are needed.

However, luminance and chroma-key techniques have a very serious limitation—there is no correlation between the foreground and background layers of the output picture in terms of movement. If in a chroma-key situation the foreground camera covering the actor in the studio moves, the background stays still. The outcome is an annoying and unnatural effect, and the fact that the background is a "fake" will be obvious to the viewer. The same will happen with movement in the background caused by camera movement of any kind in a live video source.

This is why when a still picture is used as background, the camera pointed at the actor is usually locked and does not make any movement such as pan, tilt or zoom. A virtual studio is an improvement of the chroma-key technique, but it is also much more than that.

Virtual studios were born in an attempt to overcome these constraints and were made possible by advancements in computer technology, advanced 3-D modeling and texture mapping, increased data processing speeds and newly developed pattern recognition techniques and algorithms.

The name "virtual studio" is somewhat misleading because you still need a real studio since only the scenery or set is virtual. Therefore, the name "virtual set" is probably more appropriate.

Sometimes virtual studio techniques are called "virtual reality." This name is essentially correct but it also includes applications from other, nonbroadcast fields such as computer games and simulators while virtual set is used almost exclusively for broadcast television applications.

In virtual studio systems computer generated images are used as backgrounds. The foreground camera output and the background computer-generated image are fed to a chroma-keyer that combines the two pictures. All foreground camera movements are tracked, the movement data is processed and fed to the computer that produces and renders the background picture, which is moved accordingly. If the foreground camera pans left, the background picture will move to the right and if the foreground camera zooms out, the computer that generates the background picture will perform the same effect. In this way a visually coordinated combination of foreground and background movement is created. The resulting combination looks real and it appears to the viewer that the talent is actually inside the artificial surrounding and is an integral part of it.

There are several methods of detecting and measuring the seven basic moves each camera can make. These methods differ from one manufacturer of virtual studio to another. One method is to use cameras mounted on pan and tilt heads equipped with electromechanical motion sensors on every axis of motion.

Another method is to use a fixed pattern drawn on the blue chroma-key background. A special pattern recognition system calculates every motion made by the camera through the changes of that pattern in the camera video output signal.

An additional system uses an array of infrared emitters and sensors. There is a system that uses circular bar codes mounted on the ceiling of the studio together with a pattern recognition system to calculate the camera movement. For that purpose small CCTV cameras are mounted on the bigger studio cameras and aimed at the ceiling. Some companies use more than one method for different systems or for different cameras in the same system. The different methods of motion detection will be described in detail in the following chapters.

A foreground picture can be taken from a hand held camera or from a camera mounted on a pedestal, depending on the method of motion detection in use. In some virtual set systems the number of studio cameras active in the virtual studio system is limited, in others any number of cameras can be used.

The background computer-generated image can include elements that will appear in the combined picture in front of, as well as behind the actors. Each part or object of the computer-generated environment can be defined as background or as foreground. In a case where there is a pillar in the center of the computer-generated environment defined as foreground, it will hide the actor whenever he moves "behind" the pillar, in a natural and convincing way in the combined output picture. The definition as foreground or background of the same pillar can be switched during a program to allow an actor to appear one time in front of it and another behind it.

The virtual studio technique allows the creation of new looks and designs not possible with conventional scenery building techniques using materials such as wood and metal. The virtual environment is created as computer graphics that can look like something from real life—like an ordinary living room, or something imaginary, out of this world, limited only by the imagination of those who create it.

In comparison to conventional TV scenery, a virtual set has many advantages and flexibility: the environment can be a variety of things from a static flat artwork to a live and moving multielement 3-D computer animation. One artist or designer can produce new scenery or a set during a few days using a computer. Still and live video pictures can be combined into virtual scenery, making it appear dynamic and more interesting.

There is no longer need to build, maintain, store and move around complicated and heavy scenery. An unlimited number of movements of set elements, changes in shape, color, texture and lighting can be programmed during a program. Elements such as live video screens, scoreboards, still pictures, stages, walls, pedestals, maps and any imaginary item can be manipulated in 3-D movement and 3-D space in real time, appear out of nowhere, disappear, or be a permanent part of the virtual scenery. Lines of text can fly around while changing color, texture, size and transparency. The ceiling can fly away and reveal a whole new set or world while the floor can move aside, disappear, become transparent or change color and texture.

Every element or part in the set can be changed from one thing to another and can be moved and rotated all in real time. One complete studio set can be replaced by another by a click of a mouse, while the program is on air. Since the environment the TV viewers see is not real but computer-generated, most of the time studios smaller than those necessary for a conventional set, can be used for a virtual set production. The virtual set takes care of additional subjects such as set dressing, props and complicated lighting of conventional sets in the studio. All that is needed in the TV studio is an evenly lit blue background and simple lighting for the actor or actors. All the rest is part of the computer-generated background image.

The virtual studio is not limited to in-house work only. At least one successful attempt has been made to use the virtual studio in the field simply by placing an announcer at a football game in front of a piece of blue cloth. The Virtual studio hardware was installed in the O.B. van covering the game.

By using the virtual set labor of moving around and setting up scenery can be saved, as well as storage space. There is no need to invest in materials and pay the costs of scenery builders every time new scenery has to be built.

The virtual studio is still in its infancy both technically and especially in terms of creativity. There is no doubt that in the coming years we will witness extensive progress and greater sophistication in the art of designing new virtual scenery and environments. As can be seen, the virtual studio has many virtues. There are also some problems with implementing this technology, but they are only a few and not hard to overcome.

3   What to Look for in a Virtual Studio

Before setting a meeting with a salesperson regarding the purchase of a virtual studio system, there are several questions to be prepared for. Besides the obvious question of the budget allocated for this purpose, the answers to these questions will form the beginning of a technical description of the system you need:

- Does the system have to work live on-air?
- How many cameras need to be part of the system?
- Do you use hand-held cameras in the studio?
- Do you need cameras to move in the studio or will the camera positions be completely static?
- Is there a lot of movement by performers in the studio?
- What is the size of the studio?
- What level of sophistication do you expect from the background graphics? Is 2-D enough?
- Do you have graphic artists on your staff?
- Do you have more than one studio in your facility that you would like to connect to the virtual studio system?

There are several manufacturers of virtual studio equipment and some of them offer more than one system. When shopping for a virtual studio system to fit your specific needs, many different considerations are involved. The first thing to bear in mind is perhaps what the system should not do. A good virtual studio system should not in any way restrict the way in which you operate your studio. It should not impose on you long calibration procedures whereby most of the studio staff just has to wait for it to end.

It should not interfere with work in the studio or otherwise limit the way studio staff is used in the studio production. This is especially important if you intend to use your studio as a virtual studio only part of the time while the rest of time it is intended to work as it use to before. The virtual studio system should not prevent you from moving your cameras freely in the studio while using any kind of camera support; studio pedestal, crane or a hand held camera.

You should look for a system that will allow you to use studio equipment such as cameras, teleprompters, switchers and character generators the same way with or without a virtual studio involved, as much as possible. The virtual studio system should allow performers complete freedom to move around the studio floor and should allow camera operators to follow the talent with their cameras the same as in any ordinary studio production. It is the function of the system to synchronize the movement of the computer generated 3-D graphics with the movement of the camera that is on-air at every given moment. If a proposed system is going to restrict your studio operation in any of the above mentioned ways, think very carefully before purchasing it even if its price is attractive.

Probably the most important contribution of the virtual studio system to your organization should be the ability to add to your creative, artistic and operational possibilities and freedom. Before purchasing a virtual studio, the ability of the system to grow from an entry or mid-range level to a high-end system has to be investigated.

A virtual set should increase the income from your studio space by turning a small or medium size studio into a place where "big market" productions are made and it should at the same time save scenery building, maintenance and storage costs.

There are different levels of virtual studio products. Some manufacturers such as ORAD define their products as entry-level, mid-range and high-end and some don't. RT-SET has two levels of systems to offer. Others such as Accom, Evans & Sutherland and Radamec have only one system on sale. Naturally price levels are in proportion to the performance of each system. Low-end systems will usually use computers such as the Silicon-Graphics O2, while higher level systems will use a Silicon-Graphics Onyx 2, InfinitReality. Sometimes combinations of one high-end computer and a few others are used.

There are major differences between camera tracking systems to be considered. Pattern recognition systems are more expensive but they allow you almost complete freedom to move your cameras in the studio and to use any number of cameras.

An electromechanical camera tracking systems has a price for each additional camera to be used. For each camera connected to the virtual studio system a special camera pan and tilt head, lens zoom and focus sensors have to be purchased. This kind of system usually does not allow cameras to move from place to place in a track or dolly movement and if it does, with special track sensors, the movement is very limited. When using electromechanical head sensors the camera's position has to be fixed during a virtual studio production. Cameras cannot be moved freely, hand held or otherwise. If the same cameras are used for ordinary production they can move normally. Another restriction is that a calibration of the system has to be performed before starting a virtual studio recording.

The auxiliary camera system and the infrared system also require additional equipment for each additional camera connected to the system. If you can settle for one camera in the studio in a fixed position, the matter is simple, one electro-mechanical sensor head will do. If you need the single camera to move around on a pedestal or hand-held, you need one of the other, more sophisticated systems.

If you need several free moving cameras to be hooked-up to your system you probably need a pattern recognition system. Sometimes two different camera-tracking systems are combined.

Most entry-level systems use a Silicon Graphics O2 workstation as the graphics engine. In an entry-level system, you can typically find the following capabilities:

Full capability to move background graphics in synchronization with camera movement.

- Ability to handle 2-D graphics of up to 4,096 x 4,096 pixels in real time.
- A restricted ability to render 3-D objects, at the moment some 2,000 polygons in real time. 3-D background has meaning only if a camera tracking system that can track camera position changes is used, otherwise, a 2-D background is a better option.
- Support for one or more cameras depending on the tracking system selected.
- Support of unlimited pan, tilt, zoom and focus from a fixed camera position. If a pattern recognition camera-tracking system is used, unrestricted camera movement can be performed including handheld cameras and any number of cameras can be used.
- Ability to import graphic files in a variety of popular formats.

- Possibility for easy upgrade to high-end systems by changing the graphics engine computer and adding software modules.

In more sophisticated systems many additional capabilities are to be found. Some of them are listed here. Not all of them can be found in a single system:
- Multicamera handling.
- A combination of two different camera-tracking systems.
- Ability to handle 3-D graphics and objects in real time, including 50,000 to 100,000 polygons.
- Trash-mattes—an option that allows parts of the studio background not to be covered with blue cloth or paint. The ceiling of the studio where the lights are is a good example for a place where a trash-matte is needed.
- Depth keying—tracking the position of moving performers or objects in the studio; this information is used in the graphic engine to manage the relationship between real and virtual objects.
- Depth of focus effects—an effect in which the background is defocused to create a sensation of depth in the composed picture.
- Shadow handling—shadows of real objects in the studio are reconstructed in the composed output image.
- Virtual camera functions—a viewpoint of the background from places outside the real studio created by the graphic engine. Can be mixed with real camera shots.
- Interface with external devices such as computers running tables or game statistics.
- Automatic control of audio and video delays. Used to set the correct delay needed according to the camera tracking system used.
- Automatic predesigned insertion of sound effects. Allows accurate insertion of sound effects according to movement in the background animation or movement of actors in the studio.
- Remote feed insertion—the ability to seamlessly integrate people from different locations, one in the local studio and the other in a remote setting, both located in a blue box.

If your requirements from the virtual studio system do not include live transmission such as news, you can purchase a postproduction system. Most manufacturers offer such systems: Accom offers the ELSET-post, Evans & Sutherland offer the Mindset-post, ORAD offers a special version of the CyberSet for postproduction and RT-SET offers the Larus-post.

Doing virtual studio production offline will save considerable expense and will not limit the level of graphics that can be rendered in real time. In post systems there is no need to buy high-end supercomputers such as the SGI Onyx-2. A much cheaper O2 will do the rendering frame-by-frame, according to camera tracking information and time-code gathered in the computer. After the rendering is finished, the video recorded in the studio will be composited with the rendered background graphics.

The postproduction process may take a day or two, but it will produce better photo-realistic results for less money. The resolution in the postrendering method is unlimited, and HDTV material can also be processed. Postproduction virtual studio work is best used for, but not limited to, video clips, commercials, promos, special effects and sequences.

The possibility of using a single virtual set system for several studios in the same facility or station is something to be discussed with manufacturers before purchasing. In some cases a system can be efficiently utilized for different studios in a "time sharing" scheme. Proper wiring and routing equipment needs to be installed for this kind of arrangement. However the price of such installation is very low compared to the benefits.

Components of a Virtual Studio

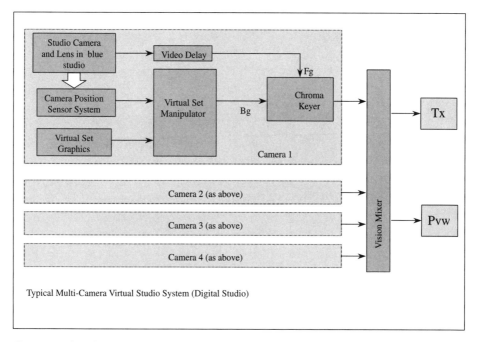

Typical Multi-Camera Virtual Studio System (Digital Studio)

Courtesy of Radamec.

Costs of virtual studio systems:

It is very complicated to provide accurate pricing information. The price of a system is composed of many components and the price of the same system can change significantly from one country to another.

Systems are usually sold not including computer hardware. What the buyer basically gets is a software license. In addition different software and hardware options can be added to the basic system, according to requirements.

Entry level and post systems that are SGI O2 or PC based range in prices from $40,000 to $130,000. Some system that use video as background instead of graphic files can be cheaper.

A basic, mid-range system that is usually based on a SGI Onyx Reality engine will cost somewhere between $90,000 and $100,000.

A high-end, basic SGI Onyx InfinitReality engine based system will cost between $180,000 and $220,000.

A single sensor pan and tilt head costs some $30,000 to $35,000.

The price of a SGI O2 computer is about $12,000.

The list price of a SGI Onyx Reality engine is some $110,000 and a deskside InfinitReality Onyx is some $180,000.

4   Virtues of Virtual

Virtual studios are still at the infancy stage but many advantages are clear to broadcasters and to all those already involved in virtual studio program production. Some of the advantages are esthetic and artistic while others relate to facilities and equipment. The artistic qualities are by far the most attractive features of virtual studio technology but other factors such as saving money are not to be ignored.

Virtual studio technology breaks all the conventions of how a television studio program should look and behave. Absolute creative freedom can be given to set designers who are no longer restricted to the design of ordinary objects and environments. Among the conventions that can be broken are some that we did not really relate to—for example, until now we were used to seeing TV programs that go from start to finish with the same scenery in the background. With virtual studio technology this can, and probably will change very fast. The set behind performers and announcers in a virtual studio production can change before our eyes during the transmission of the program many times and in many ways. Virtual objects which are parts of the virtual set or the complete set can change color, shape, transparency, function and any other property they may have. These changes can be carried out in relation to certain events in the program, or as a continuous process. Until now if there was a TV screen in the set, it would usually look like one. From now on there is no reason why walls or the floor of the set cannot become the live video image. A screen can also float in mid-air, located and moving in 3-D space. Obviously the artistic and creative possibilities are enormous.

Making a new set for a program is much cheaper and faster than before. Renewing a set of an existing program does not take as much effort as with ordinary hard scenery.

Examples of virtual sets, courtesy of ORAD.

It is not only cheaper to make a virtual set, but it allows you to make "impossible" sets, things that you simply cannot build with conventional building materials such as metal and plywood. A futuristic, hi-tech look can be easily given to programs. Besides programs, virtual sets are very suitable for making music clips, promos and commercials.

Virtual sets do not require large storage areas and certainly need no maintenance. Storage space in urban areas is very expensive and the use of virtual sets can reduce real-estate expenses. There is no need to carry the scenery into the studio, to erect it before every shooting session, take it apart afterwards, and carry it to the storage area. A complete, large set can be stored on a CD. Materials such as wood, metal, glass, plastics and paint are no longer needed.

The use of virtual sets saves money in many different ways. Studio efficiency and productivity becomes much higher. In studios from which several different programs are aired, a set change from one program to another takes a matter of seconds, with no hard labor involved. Stagehands do not have to move around heavy scenery, and complicated lighting changes are not needed. The same basic lighting will do for several kinds of virtual environments.

A virtual set can appear many times bigger than the actual studio space it is shot in. The typical virtual studio is what in broadcasting is defined as a small, not even medium, size studio. An environment of a large, 90 feet long, 2-story high news studio can actually be produced in a small, 15 feet long studio and even less, depending on the number of performers and the amount of movement on the studio floor. Using smaller studios reduces air condition, lighting and maintenance costs. A virtual set of a huge news studio, with video walls, many picture monitors, VCRs, staircases, huge maps and logos, can be shot in a relatively small studio.

We are in the era where more and more stations are converting to high definition television and have to recondition hard sets to confirm with the much higher resolution of HDTV. Several virtual studio systems today can operate in a HDTV environment and save set renovation costs.

The process of "building" a virtual set allows freedom to do things that were never before possible in real sets. During the implementation of the set design, you can change your mind and make as many changes as you want. No valuable materials such as plywood and paint will be wasted. The set can be checked in the studio even before it is completely ready with textures and lighting effects. Even when the set is finished, changes can be easily made. Several versions of the same set can be made before the production starts and versions can be easily switched within seconds. For example the same set can be made with a daylight version, a twilight version and a night version.

At least one news station uses virtual studio technology to produce several news programs a day, each one looks different, all look great, but they all come from the same small studio, on the same day.

Examples of virtual sets, courtesy of ORAD.

Virtual set technology allows the producer to use sets that are either too expensive to build, too dangerous to get to, or exist only in the wild imagination of an innovative scriptwriter. It is possible to make in advance a series of sets and switch between them during production in the studio as the plot progresses and requires a different "location." This method of operation can enrich the program's look. Set changes can be performed in a fraction of the time usually needed for a conventional set change. Virtual studio systems are easy to install. A typical installation of a new system will take no longer than two working days.

A virtual studio system can serve any number of studios in the same building or even remotes. The same single system can be routed to produce a children's program in studio A in the morning, do a talk-show in studio B in the afternoon and still manage to do the news in the evening with no problem at all.

Several virtual set systems can be installed in parallel, in the same studio and each produce a different look and different background for the same performers or announcers in the same studio. The performance of virtual studio technology is constantly improving, while the technical limitations it imposes on the production are becoming fewer.

New features are added to virtual studio systems at a rate typical of the computer industry, but not really known in the broadcast equipment business. Growth of graphic-engines power allows virtual sets to become more complex and photo-realistic. As more and more virtual studio productions are made, experience is gathered among graphic designers and artists and sets are becoming more convincing and richer in content and visual effects. Some companies offer off-the-shelf or tailor-made designs of sets for every purpose.

Finally, virtual studio technology has come to a point where it can no longer be ignored. The artistic, practical and financial benefits require no additional proof. From new kinds of productions and programs that are successfully performed with virtual studio systems, we can conclude that virtual studio is here to stay.

A virtual set used for an NAB exhibition, courtesy of ORAD.

Examples of virtual sets, courtesy of Accom.

Examples of virtual sets, courtesy of ORAD.

5   What Makes a Virtual
Set Convincing

A virtual studio environment is a combination of two components. The first one is the real studio, with the blue or green cyclorama in the background and performers who operate in the studio in front of the cameras. The second part is the computer-generated neighborhood that includes the background and sometimes also foreground items at the same time. This neighborhood is a part of a display that exists only on picture monitors or TV screens. If you turn off the computer, the neighborhood vanishes.

Merging between these two totally different entities is the essence of virtual studio. Obviously such a marriage is not easily attained. A great deal of planning and a considerable amount of high-end equipment and software is involved. The purpose of a virtual set project is to create and display to the viewer a unified entity with the best of these two worlds. Actors, announcers and interviewees should be immersed in computer-generated surroundings in the most natural way. The human eye is a precision instrument that is not easily fooled. Minor changes or inconsistencies in position, lighting or color will be disturbing even to the untrained eye.

Virtual sets are divided into two families. One is a set that endeavors to display a neighborhood that is familiar to us such as a kitchen or the inside of a train. The other kind of set is the creation of an imaginary surrounding, something we have not seen before and this is where a virtual studio production can really show its capabilities and potential.

There are several factors that make a convincing composition between real performers and a virtual environment. First of all, the computer-generated background itself, with no connection to anything else must look convincing. Real-life surroundings are more difficult to make since everyone knows what a kitchen looks like. Every detail must be accurately made for the whole scene to be convincing. Imaginary neighborhoods are less demanding and give more freedom to the artist. The use of real items such as furniture and other household items placed in the studio can add reality to the virtual set. Creation of such small items as part of a virtual set is time consuming and makes the graphics files much larger. This in turn puts an extra burden on the graphic engines, which are pushed to their limits as it is. The presence of real furniture in the studio will also improve an actor's orientation in the set.

The right correlation between performers in the studio and the computer-generated background is another important factor. This is one of the difficult issues to deal with, especially when there is movement of performers in studio or movement in the computer generated background or both. Obviously the more movement there is in the foreground and background, the more complicated lighting will be. Each movement in the studio should be carefully planned so that it will interact correctly with virtual objects in the 3-D background animation. If a "collision" occurs between a virtual object and a real actor, for instance, if an actor walks through a virtual brick wall, the realism of the set is compromised for the rest of the program.

Lighting and shadows are other complicated issues to deal with. In everyday life we do not pay too much attention to light, shadows and reflections. However, if in a virtual set situation a light casts a shadow the wrong way, or reflects in an odd way from a glass surface, we will notice it immediately, and it will diminish the realism of the set. Three different sets of lighting and shadows exist in a virtual studio environment, the lighting of the blue background in the studio, the lighting of performers in the studio and lighting effects within the 3-D image. The lighting of the blue background is not part of the composed picture and is used only to create an even background which the chroma-keyer will replace with the computer-generated artwork. This lighting is of a more technical nature, even though it is definitely an art form to make good cyclorama lighting.

Success in creating good lighting requires planning and close coordination between the lighting director of the studio and the graphic designer of the virtual set. It is the right blending of studio lighting and lighting effects in the background that will impart a convincing, photo-realistic look to the composed output of the system.

Shadows are also important to create a photo-realistic result. Shadows cast by live actors on the blue studio background can be reconstructed on the composited image. Reflections of real objects from the floor in places where the virtual floor is supposed to be glossy can be achieved by placing reflecting material on the studio floor.

Since our TV screen is flat and delivers only a two-dimensional picture, conveying a perception of depth is not easily achieved. In conventional television one of the things that adds to this perception is the difference in sharpness between foreground and background. This difference occurs in conventional television when the camera is focused on a near object while the background further away is out of focus. The amount of defocus depends on the distances from the camera lens and on iris opening, which is dependent on the amount of light in the studio.

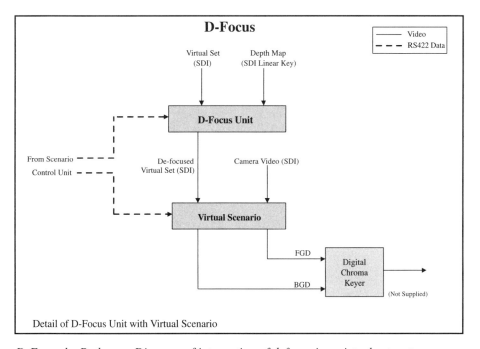

D-Focus by Radamec. Diagram of integration of defocus in a virtual set system.

In a virtual set this situation does not occur naturally. The camera is focused on actors while the background comes from the computer, in full sharpness, at all times. Advanced virtual studio systems such as Accom's ELSET-LIVE and ORAD's Cyberset-O address these issues and provide tools for depth of field effects. Special algorithms and data from electromechanical sensors in the camera lens are used to defocus the virtual background when the lens focus is pulled back.

The quality and realism of the set are in the hands of the graphic designer and those who implement his ideas, but there are technological limitations to be dealt with. To a very large extent the reality of virtual set programs is determined by the ability of the graphic engines to render highly detailed sets, with a large count of polygons in the 3-D animation, texture mapping and lighting effects. Rendering the set in real time according to foreground camera movement makes it necessary to use high-end, expensive supercomputers. Even so the power of existing graphic engines is not always enough.

Certain techniques are used to reduce the number of polygons in 3-D animations and the amount of resolution needed in textures. Some effects such as complex ray tracing that add realism can be rendered only offline. The need to render sophisticated 3-D graphics in real time imposes serious limitations. A background of an exterior landscape for example, is not possible to render live at this time. The fine detail of leaves and grass or detail of buildings in a large city cannot be handled even by the most advanced currently available hardware. The closest thing to such exteriors is a still picture of an exterior view mapped onto a window in an interior set.

The virtual studio industry is waiting for a newer generation of high-end graphic computers. There is much to be desired in this area, and a quantum leap in computer performance is something that would enable all aspects of virtual studio production to make significant strides forward.

6   Programs Suitable for Virtual Studio Use

What kind of programs can I do with a virtual studio system? This is a question most TV producers and station managers ask. Well, the answer depends on whom you're asking. Most salespeople of virtual studio manufacturers will say "with our systems you can do any kind of program you want."

This answer is mostly true. There are no rules that state what kind of programs you can or cannot do. It largely depends on the creativity of producers and engineers, and the willingness of virtual studio manufacturers to create tailor-made solutions. A variety of programs is being produced every day. At the top of the list you will find news, weather and election coverage. Talk shows with a limited number of participants are next followed by game shows, drama, and musical programs. Educational programs also lend themselves very well to virtual studio production. Children's programs are also being made. Some large corporations such as General Motors use virtual studio technology to produce instructional programs for internal use.

However, there are some limitations of the virtual studio that will probably influence such decisions. The size of studios used in virtual studio productions is usually not larger and most of the time much smaller than 3,000 square feet. This is due to limitations of camera tracking systems, especially those that deal with position rather than orientation. If we take, for example, an infrared system, the larger the studio area, the more infrared cameras or detectors will be needed and more sophisticated software will be needed to process the data from the detectors.

Another limitation is the number of people on the set. It is difficult to properly light and control the movement of more than ten or fifteen people for chroma-key. Programs with a large audience in the studio will be difficult to make.

Besides the size of studio and the number of people in the studio, there are no prominent limitations. Producers are competing to see who can use virtual studio technology in the most innovative and creative manner.

Camera movement tracking systems become less limiting and newer versions that allow the use of larger spaces are frequently introduced.

Following are some examples of virtual studio projects that demonstrate the possibilities of the technology:

The Florida's News Channel (FNC) which is a news supplier to a variety of channels, has built a cutting-edge facility. In order to transmit a different newscast every few hours, to eight different affiliates each with its own logo in the set, normally requires an enormous amount of facilities. At FNC a single virtual studio does the job. Sets are changed within a few seconds. No stage hands and no realignment of the lighting are needed. In this case ORAD has produced a tailor-made solution where, for each channel, there is an O2 computer that renders the output slightly differently. This is a solution that made the whole operation possible in technical and economical terms.

WDR in Germany did a series called *City Express*. This is a drama that took place in a moving train. To shoot such a drama series in a real moving train would be extremely complicated and expensive. At WDR they came up with an original and rather complicated solution. Several wagons were placed with one side open in a large studio. Every scene was shot from four different angles. One of the problems was to have a realistic view from the windows in a supposedly moving train. Views from a real moving train window were shot each from four different angles. The windows of the train cars in the studio were painted chroma-key green.

When scenes in the studio are shot each camera is connected to a virtual studio system. The green background in the car windows is replaced with the scenes shot outside the studio. A video server plays all four live scenery viewpoints simultaneously. Cuts can be made between outputs of the four virtual studio systems, each having a different viewpoint of the scene. Obviously each background accurately follows the camera orientation and zoom. For this project ORAD installed special DVE software into the DVP units to allow long smooth zooms with no pixelation and flickering effects.

Sometimes the train stops at stations which are virtual sets. Above each window there is a video projector that projects a defocused picture of the outside view onto the actors in the car so that the changing light will reflect from their face and add realism to the scene.

WDR has a studio equipped with a triple CyberSet-O system. Each of the three camera channels is a complete virtual set system that contains a separate Onyx 2. In the studio a multipanel system is used where three pattern recognition grids are located in the studio. This allows cameras a viewing sector of some 270 degrees. The studio is used for a daily magazine that deals every day with another subject such as health, cooking, travel, and economics. The studio also contains seats for an audience. The arrangement allows for use of real and virtual sets in the same program.

LRP, a New York production house, needed to add actors and information into old b/w commercials. Instead of having to reconstruct and reshoot the old commercials, they were used as background in a virtual studio. Actors were positioned in the foreground (in b/w as well) and a small amount of defocus of the background added to the feeling of reality. Limited movement was possible because of the limited resolution of the video background, but it was enough to bind the video background and actors in the foreground into one entity. A large amount of money was saved in the process.

NHK in Japan has a music program in HDTV with a small orchestra or quartet playing in the studio. To make things more interesting a round revolving stage was placed in the studio. The orchestra is placed on the stage and stage movement is synchronized with the movement of the background. A camera that takes the long shot is located on crane that moves up and down, while the stage is revolving and the background is moving. The result is it seams that as if the crane is doing a 360 degree movement around the players. The whole thing is shot in a studio, which is some 800 sq. feet in size. The outcome can give an impression of a huge space, depending on the background graphics used.

Madison Square Garden (MSG) in New York uses a studio of some 400 sq. feet for sports events coverage. A virtual studio system is installed and in the studio there is a table and chair for the sports reporter and a blue chromakey background. The virtual studio system was purchased with a set of different backgrounds. MSG produces sports segments for different clients and for each client there is the appropriate background file. A reporter comes into the studio, the proper background is loaded into the virtual studio system and a segment is recorded or transmitted live. This process is repeated many times a day, and a very small staff operates the system. In this case as in many others, the utilization of the studio is many times more efficient than is possible with ordinary scenery.

POLSAT of Poland had a problem. They had to provide a full day's transmission from two small studios and with a limited budget. After installation of virtual studio systems the problem was solved. The two studios are used for a wide variety of programs such as news, talk shows and children's programs. Several programs are produced in each studio every day, some of them live. With the virtual systems the two small studios are able to produce enough content to fill the stations' needs, something which was not possible before.

BBC's Omnibus is a flagship arts program. It is renowned for it's innovation and quality and for many performances created specially for the program. In 1998 a program about the work of the Royal Ballet dancer Darcey Bussell was scheduled. The initial plan was to produce a program in which the famous dancer would perform using traditional methods three solo roles, in addition to archival footage. Under normal circumstances, three large, complex sets had to be built: Swan Lake, La Bayadere and Cinderella. It became clear that both the budget and time constraints exceeded the limitation of such an art documentary. Then arose the idea to use virtual sets. Virtual Video Studios in London were recruited to do the job, using an Evans & Sutherland MindSet system. Suddenly the large budgets needed for the design and construction of the sets shrunk. All three sets were created in two weeks. The sequences were shot on a 45-foot long stage, with a blue background and a dance floor borrowed from a London dance company. The lighting for the set was part of the background graphics, so all that remained was to light the dancer. Each sequence was shot three times, with a single camera, for wide, medium and narrow shots. Changing from one set to another and making some special effects lighting changes took as long as it took for the dancer to change costume.

The outcome was stunning. This production proved that virtual studio technology can be successfully used for dance, opera and other performing arts production for television. It can save money and add artistic freedom at the same time.

One of the milestones of children's programs produced with the aid of virtual studio technology is **Disney's *One Saturday Morning*** aired weekly by ABC. An Accom Elset virtual studio system using three SGI Onyx Infinite Reality workstations was chosen to do the job. For the virtual set version of the show a huge colorful 3-D virtual set was built with a roller coaster traveling through it. Among other things there was a 30-foot diameter cereal bowl floating 15 feet above the stage floor and a 1,200 sq. foot video monitor made of stone that flies in. All of that was not, of course, possible to create with real scenery.

The initial set built was much too large to be handled live by the Onyx Infinite Reality computer used. After dividing the large set into smaller rooms and camera positions and some polygon-geometry changes the problem was solved.

The stage was 4,000 sq. feet large and held some 30 people—children on skateboards, bicycles and bumper-cars that moved on the stage floor. Three cameras were used, one mounted on a pedestal, one on a dolly and one on a crane. A green chroma-key background was chosen to avoid problems with common clothes worn by children such as blue jeans. An average of some 100 minutes of live action composed with virtual background were recorded per day.

It seems that today whenever a producer sets his mind to do a new production the virtual way, the right solutions will be found, and the production will become a reality.

Examples of virtual sets, courtesy of ORAD.

7 Limitations of Virtual Studios

Virtual studio is a relatively new technology. Relying heavily on high-end computer technology, the virtual set, or background is a 2-D or 3-D graphic. The quality of the graphics file determines the overall quality and look of the composed TV program.

Both 2-D and 3-D graphics have limitations when used as backgrounds for a TV program. Entry level, real time systems use 2-D backgrounds. These 2-D backgrounds use various techniques to create a feeling of depth. In this system, cameras in the studio must stay in one place and not change their position during the program. If a camera moves, the fact that the background is flat will be revealed to viewers and the set will lose its credibility. Fairly convincing sets can be made using high quality 2-D graphics. However, the ultimate illusion of reality is obtained by using 3-D virtual sets. 3-D sets allow, and even require, movement of cameras in the studio's 3-D space. If the camera in a 3-D virtual set does not move, you can use a much simpler 2-D graphics system and get the same visual effect.

Using 3-D graphics in real time requires several expensive technologies. Supercomputers such as the Silicon Graphics Onyx2 are needed to render graphics at the TV field rate. Sophisticated camera tracking systems are needed to track camera movement in eight degrees of freedom. This is to make just one channel of virtual studio.

If the requirement is for a system that allows live dissolves or other transitions between camera channels, an additional supercomputer is needed. A preview option requires another computer, usually at the level of an O2. A two channel 3-D online system with preview becomes a considerably expensive assemblage.

Virtual sets are divided into two categories—sets that look like something real and familiar such as a living room or bar, and sets that doesn't look like anything we know and are completely imaginary.

With the first category there is still much to be desired. High quality 3-D graphics include a large number of polygons, textures, and various effects such as ray tracing, morphing and anti-aliasing. Rendering all that live is not currently possible even with the most powerful graphic workstations. To get a photo-realistic result a careful balance and compromise between the different ingredients in the 3-D artwork is needed. It also involves a few tricks of the trade to get a convincing set. A sufficient degree of realism can be achieved, but it is not easy and requires considerable experience and know-how. These problems disappear with offline work, but some productions such as newscasts must work live. Imaginary virtual sets cause less of a problem. The question of photo-realism is obviously less significant.

Another problem with virtual sets is the working conditions in the studio. Performers act most of the time in an empty blue space. The interaction with nonexistent scenery is difficult. Care must be taken so that performers will not collide with virtual 3-D objects in the studio. The only way to coordinate movement is to rehearse while using picture monitors in the studio displaying composed studio output. This situation is not new and is well known from conventional chroma-key studio work.

Virtual studio technology requires personnel not always available in TV stations or production houses. A specially trained operator, as an integral part of the studio crew, is needed to handle the virtual studio system during production. There is also the question of maintenance of the computers and software. The software is partly standard and partly specialized. Most computers used are high-end graphic workstations, usually not standard equipment in broadcasting. Set design and graphics work has to be done by a skilled person. This person can be a staff member or from an external service provider.

The camera tracking system used imposes some limitations on a virtual studio system. A pattern recognition system limits the shooting sector a camera can cover. It has to see at least a small part of the grid that is on the studio wall at all times. If the camera exceeds this limit the system will loose its orientation and freeze until the camera is again pointed at the grid.

Electromechanical camera tracking systems are very good at measuring orientation angles, but when it comes to camera movement in the 3-D studio-space they have a serious limitation. Auxiliary camera and infrared systems impose limitations on the studio size and height. Studios that are too large are a problem and so are studios with a very low ceiling. Usually two camera tracking systems are combined to minimize limitations.

Limitations of current virtual studio systems must not be ignored nor should they be a deterrent. Knowing the limitations, successful program production can take place within the known parameters. Every year advancements in virtual studio technology make systems more straightforward and less limiting. Current systems already allow a high degree of creativity and innovation in program production.

8 Management Attitudes to Virtual Studios

Television managers and producers worldwide are under a lot of pressure. New cable, DBS and terrestrial channels flourish everywhere. Ratings are dropping, bringing down program budgets. Due to the wide variety of channels, audiences become more selective and demanding.

There is a constant search for more attractive and innovative content and form, in order to compete with other stations. Producers are required to do more for less, and are in a consistent pursuit after more cost-effective program ideas. Virtual studio technology is a timely step in the right direction. It has come a long way in the few last years, with performance and ease of use dramatically improved.

Until a few years ago the entry fee to the virtual studio exclusive club was some $500,000. At such price levels even those managers who could see the benefits in terms of monetary savings and improved creative freedom, felt uneasy about taking the plunge. The technology was not sufficiently proven, and the return on the investment wasn't certain.

Today the entry fee is in the neighborhood of $100,000 and the technology is mature enough to provide satisfactory and predictable results. Entry level systems can be purchased at the price of a single studio camera and can later be upgraded. It is becoming something even relatively small television facilities can afford. Managers and decision makers in the television industry should know that virtual studios work, and work well.

Some of the latest virtual studio technology evolved when several companies that were in the business of making flight simulators looked for ways to develop new products and markets. These companies had a wealth of know-how in tracking objects in 3-D space and rendering 3-D graphics in real time. The similarity between these two applications is great, the same high-end graphic engines and the same motion detection are used. Implementation may be relatively new but the technology is proven and in widespread use.

Virtual sets are utilized in many kinds of productions both offline and live with news and weather being at the top of the list. Sporting events, talk shows, drama, dance, music clips and children's programs also use virtual set technology effectively. Special effects can also be made quickly and easily with virtual studio technology.

In terms of the economics of program making, it enables production of programs with lower budgets. An artist can create a new set in a few working days. To make a new set for a virtual studio production takes the same effort it takes to create a model of a conventional, hard set. Several sets or several variations of the same set can be made for the same program and can then be switched during production to enrich the appearance of the program. No storage space is needed for virtual sets. Several sets can be stored on a single CD.

The first brave managers that invested in virtual studio were regarded with some degree of pity. This is no longer the case. Several such managers have proved that the technology can be put to work in ways that increase productivity of existing facilities to a degree not possible before. One of the best examples is a news operation in Florida that simultaneously produces six different output channels from the same studio, with the same virtual studio system.

There is no dispute about the fact that virtual studio has its problems. The work of performers in the blue box in relation to a virtual, not physically existent environment, takes getting used to. The photo-realistic qualities of virtual studio today leaves something to be desired. Nevertheless, the virtual studio technology has matured to a degree where it must be taken into account when considering innovative and cost-effective ways of program making. You should take advantage of it, before your competitors will. Virtual studio technology is used for almost every kind of TV program. In checking the possibilities for purchasing a virtual studio system, it is recommended to contact manufacturers of such technology and explain the needs and expectations you have from a system. Some of the manufacturers have been involved in tens of productions and have gathered considerable experience. They will be able to tell you if an idea is feasible or not and what it involves. Some manufacturers can provide only a single product while others offer several levels. Virtual studio systems can be configured to fit special needs of a program or station. Options such as dissolve, preview and live inputs to the system, and the number of cameras employed all have an effect on system's price and performance.

If live programming is not one of your requirements for the system, you can use a low cost, postproduction virtual studio system that will produce high-end results. Such systems are not restricted in terms of graphics quality as the real time systems are, and can also work in HDTV.

A virtual studio system provides an effective means to make creative, "affluent looking" programs with modest resources. Sets can be frequently and easily changed each time to provide a fresh look for the program.

In terms of personnel, usually one new person is needed on the studio staff to set-up and operate the system. On the other hand, stagehands and scenery builders will be less in demand.

The introduction of virtual studio technology is a golden opportunity to be more innovative, creative, competitive and cost-effective all at the same time.

Examples of virtual sets, courtesy of Accom.

9　The Production Design Stage

The virtual set allows you to produce scenery that will break all conventions and laws of nature. It allows you to enter an enchanted world that is nothing like what we knew before. Scriptwriters and art directors will find the almost limitless nature of the virtual set challenging and stimulating.

However, 2-D or 3-D artwork that is to become a virtual set, does not make a program. The idea behind the virtual studio is not to replace a conventional set of a living room with a virtual living room that looks exactly the same. The idea is to break out of conventional boundaries to create television programs with a whole new look and concept.

As in any other complex job, good planning of the program will save a lot of time and aggravation, not to mention money. The planning process should start from the idea or concept of the program. The concept should be a good combination of content and form. A magnificent virtual set alone will not keep the audience tuned to your station for a long time. The general nature and look of the set must be an integral part of the script.

The following are some of the subjects in a virtual studio production that are different from an ordinary production:

- A real solid set is not necessary, and thus all the costs of planning, building and maintaining of such a set can be saved. Normally in a single program the price of building the scenery can be some 30 to 40% of the program's budget. In a series, the building cost is divided by the number of episodes, but storage and maintenance costs are added. In a virtual set these costs are saved. What we have instead is the cost of the graphical designer's work as well as the cost of purchasing or renting/leasing the necessary graphics workstations, according to the particular configuration required.

- More than one background or set can be prepared, and easily switched during production. This can enrich the look of the program.
- Even though it is a virtual set production, using real furniture and household objects in the studio will increase performer's orientation, lack of which can be a problem in an empty blue or green space. It will also add realism to set.
- Making a simple 2-D or 3-D virtual set background can take 2 to 3 working days of an experienced artist.
- Making a complex, state of the art 3-D set utilizing a rich variety of effects and textures, will take some 10 to 12 working days of the same artist.
  It is recommended to plan in advance who will prepare the background artwork—whether it is going to be someone from within the organization or an outside company. It will probably be more expensive to hire an outside company to do the job.
- The lighting director should be involved in the planning process from the early stages. The lighting of performers in the studio should mach the lighting and atmosphere in the virtual background. Also the lighting director should be aware of movement on the set as well as location of virtual and real objects on the set.
- It is essential that the lighting director have considerable experience in chroma-key work.
- The studios used with virtual sets can usually be much smaller. The set can be made to appear very large. This makes the production less expensive, however limitations of the number of participants in the program and movement of performers in the studio have to be carefully checked. It is best to have at least six feet of empty space between actors and cyclorama in the studio. This will make the work of the lighting director much easier.
- Every scene has to be storyboarded, including talent movement and camera angles and position. This will save expensive studio time.
- Coordination between movement of actors in the studio space and movement of the background 3-D animation requires good planning and coordination between the background designer and the director.
- Choose which mode of rendering will best suit your needs and the system you have: Prerendered 2-D, 3-D real-time rendering or offline, postrendering. Make the decision well ahead to allow sufficient time for the preparation of the background. If your program is aired live, then offline rendering is out of the question. If your company or organizations owns a virtual stu-

dio system, obviously you will probably have to use it as it is. If you are shopping for studio services, than you can decide if you want a 2-D or 3-D system.

- When making the background artwork remember that when the cameras move the background moves accordingly, therefore the background should be much larger than the initial framing.
- Allow enough time for rehearsals and checking of all talent movements in correlation to the background especially if virtual studio production is new to the studio staff.

Virtual studio technology brings many new possibilities, but it also brings added technical complexity. Apart from the efforts involved in building and storing a conventional set, a virtual studio production will require at least the same amount of manpower and skills to make. Shooting in a "blue box" has always had its problems and in addition to them high-end computers and software have to be operated in the studio. Of course, as experience is acquired, things in the studio will move more smoothly.

Left—R T Set's Hawkeye.
Below—Mobile control console.

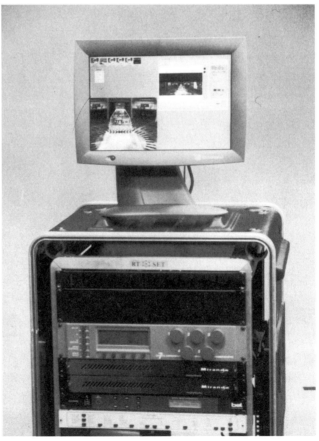

10   Technical Overview of Virtual Studio Systems

The virtual studio technology is a modern evolution of the old chroma-key technique. In simple chroma-key the blue or green background is removed from the camera output picture and another background picture is inserted instead. This function is done by the chroma-keyer and in modern virtual studio systems this is done the same way. A chroma-keyer that is part of the studio vision mixer or a stand-alone unit can be used.

In ordinary chroma-key the camera is locked and cannot be moved from place. The composition of a steady background and a moving foreground causes an odd and unnatural effect used usually only in music clips. In a virtual set arrangement the background will follow any movement made by the camera with great accuracy. The precision usually quoted by manufacturers is half a pixel. This means that no shift at all will take place between the foreground and the background. The precise linkage between the foreground that is the real world and the background, which is a virtual world, is referred to in virtual set systems as registration.

Most of the equipment used in a virtual studio system is standard broadcast equipment, the kind used in every TV station or facility. In addition, some additional hardware and software is used. The installation of a virtual studio system usually takes no more than a day or two. Being digital, systems require that digital camera signals be connected to it. In case of an analog studio, RGB to SDI converters should be installed. A converter from SDI to whatever format is used in studio other than SDI has to be installed, one for every output of the system. In digital studios the installation is more straightforward.

The heart of the system is a supercomputer that generates the background graphics and renders the changes needed in the background according to foreground camera movement.

Camera movement is measured at the field rate, which means 50 or 60 times each second. This also means that the computer has to produce a new version of the background according to a new viewpoint every 1/60 of a second if the camera moves. The changes in background between one field and the next one can be none or great, depending if the camera moves, and if it moves, how fast. It can also be a completely different viewpoint of the background when a cut between studio cameras is made. The ability to render the background at field rate is referred to in virtual studio systems as real time.

The more realistic and rich in detail the background will be, the more difficult it will be for the graphics engine to render changes in real time. Today's top of the line supercomputers can do the job but with a limited amount of polygons, texture and effects. The supercomputer is the most expensive piece of hardware one must purchase to construct a virtual studio system. Of course, this is true only if what you are after is a real time, live on-air system such as in news production. If you can manage with an offline system for productions such as music clips or commercials you can use a much cheaper computer and run graphics that are as complex as you like.

Most manufacturers build their products based on Silicon Graphics computers as platforms. For an online system you need something of the magnitude of an Onyx 2 Reality or an InfinitReality2 computer. The latter is a machine that can render some 13 million polygons per second.

The other subsystem to be added to the studio is a camera tracking system. There are several such systems, each with its pros and cons. Some systems are hardware based and require special pan and tilt heads that measure camera orientation by means of electromechanical sensors for each camera. A zoom and focus sensor unit is attached to the gear of each lens. These systems send data to the computer via RS-232 or RS-422 serial communication. Every camera involved in the production needs to be fitted with the same equipment.

A distinct disadvantage of the electromechanic system is the inability to deliver the position of the camera, which means that the camera must be used from a fixed position and can only perform pan, tilt and zoom motions.

When a multi-camera layout is used there is a need to switch the right camera tracking signal to the computer. A standard PC can do this with a multi-port communications card.

Some other camera tracking systems are more sophisticated and measure the position of the camera as well. Such systems require different hardware and wiring. Infrared systems use small cameras installed in the studio ceiling and infrared LEDs installed on cameras.

The more sophisticated the camera tracking system is, the more time it takes to calculate camera-tracking data. Current systems need up to 4 frames for the process.

The output of the processor is fed to the computer that handles the graphics via parallel communication. Sometimes two kinds of camera tracking systems are used, to create a more flexible, accurate and fault proof system.

The graphic-engine renders the background according to camera tracking data in real time and after rendering the background, graphics are fed to the background input of the chroma-keyer.

CYBERSET *BASIC* CONFIGURATION

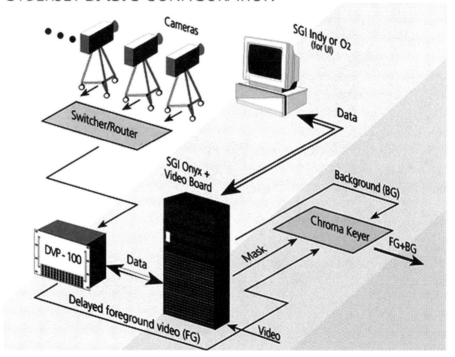

Courtesy of ORAD.

The camera on-air is connected to the foreground input of the chroma-keyer. This means that the rendered graphics, that are used as background, will enter the chroma-keyer a few frames late. To compensate, a video delay line has to be inserted in the video path between the camera and the chroma-keyer. The delay time needs to be adjusted to the exact delay created by the camera tracking system. It is best to consult the manufacturer regarding the exact delay time created in each system.

All audio has to be delayed as well, whether it comes from sound sources such as CDs and VCRs or from microphones in the studio. Delayed audio is sent to all studio outputs except the public address system in the studio, where it could cause confusion to performers, as well as damaging echo effects. Audio delay units are usually installed in the studio audio control room where the sound engineer has control over the length of the delay. Within a few years most of the virtual set systems will be able to do all data processing in a duration of less than one field, which will make delay lines in the system unnecessary.

CYBERSET E-
PATTERN RECOGNITION CONFIGURATION

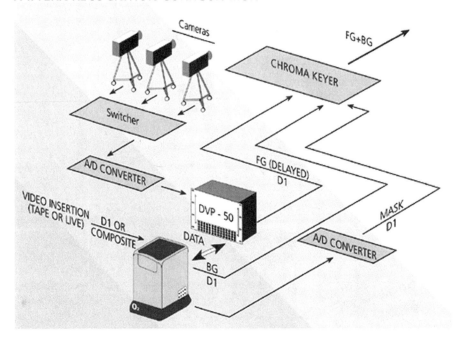

Courtesy of ORAD.

High quality chroma-keyers have to be used for best results. Some manufacturers can do with any digital chroma-keyer and others insist on Ultimatte 7 or higher. For preview channels, low cost chroma-keyers can be used.

Virtual studio systems can be used in a variety of configurations. The simplest form is a single camera without preview. Preview is an option in some systems and in some others it is part of every configuration. Adding cameras makes the system more complex, but not always. Pattern-recognition based systems require no additional equipment for every additional camera.

A dissolve option between cameras is the most costly and complicated lay-out. To have such an option two complete parallel systems each with its own graphic-engine, system software, chroma-keyer and delay lines are needed. The two parallel output signals are then fed to the studio production switcher, where a mix, wipe or any other transition or superimposition may take place.

If more than two cameras need the option to be mixed, a router can be used to switch camera signals to the input of each channel of the system, according

Proposed CyberSet O Block Diagram

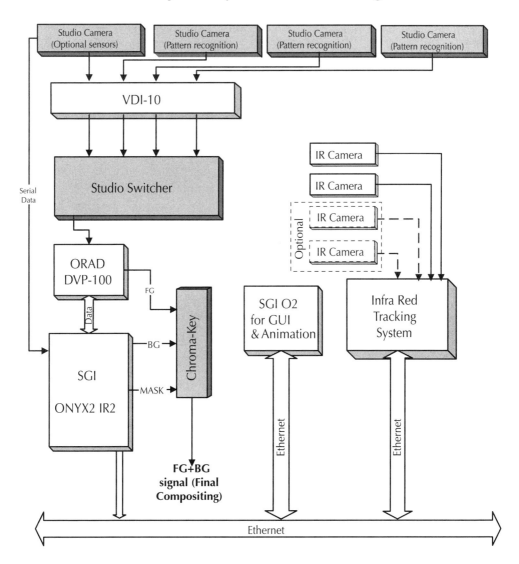

Courtesy of ORAD.

to need. If a preview option needs to be added, a third channel is constructed using a relatively low cost computer such as an O2.

A virtual studio system as complicated as it may seem, is relatively simple in terms of its interconnection to the existing studio. Any experienced broadcast engineer will be able to connect the system or service it.

The more complicated part in setting up a system is installing the different specialized software modules on the system computers and running the communications properly between the different computers and camera tracking devices. An Ethernet network usually interconnects computers in the systems. Camera tracking data is usually carried by RS-422 communications. Some camera tracking systems require specialized initial adjustment and calibration.

Usually the standard computer hardware and software is purchased directly by the end-user, according to a list provided by the virtual studio system manufacturer. The system manufacturer's engineers will install the computers together with the rest of the virtual studio system. Usually one week is taken to install the system, test it and do necessary training for the studio staff.

Proposed CyberSet E Block Diagram

Courtesy of ORAD.

11   2-D or 3-D?

Our world is three-dimensional. The television screen is flat and has only two dimensions. In the television studio performers can move in 3-D space. Cameras in the studio can move in 3-D space. 2-D backgrounds are easy to handle. 3-D animation is intricate. How do we deal with all these factors when shopping for a virtual studio system?

To achieve a convincing virtual background, it is best to use 3-D graphics composited with signals coming from cameras that move in the studio freely. To convey to viewers the sensation of depth and realism, the cameras should change not only their orientation but their position as well. If in a virtual set a handheld camera or a Steadicam is used and camera movement follows the action in the studio, good 3-D artwork rendered in the background will make the perfect illusion. The human eye, being very sensitive to any imperfection, will be satisfied.

If a 3-D background is used and cameras do not move in the 3-D studio space, viewers will not notice that the background has depth, instead it will look flat. In such a case there is no justification to purchase an expensive 3-D real-time rendering workstation.

Entry level virtual studio systems use only 2-D backgrounds. These systems use relatively low cost computers, typically Silicon Graphics O2 that are not able to render 3-D in real time. Some techniques and tricks can be used to add a sensation of depth to a 2-D set. In such cases camera-tracking systems can also be more simple and low cost. Since the cameras do not move from place, only the orientation angles and zoom/focus position have to be measured, and not the position of the camera. The background graphics being a 2-D drawing is relatively simple to make. 2-D graphics are prerendered and composed with the foreground picture by means of the chroma-keyer.

Surveys show that in today's everyday TV production, 90% of camera shots in the studio do not include camera position changes. This means that movements such as dolly, crab, pedestal up/down and also cranes, handheld cameras and Steadicam systems are used in only 10% of the shots.

Apparently, this study supports the argument that 2-D systems are adequate and 3-D systems with the expensive supercomputers needed are not essential. However, as in many other areas in our lives, this is a case where for an added 20% of quality, 80% of the product price is paid.

Using 2-D graphics as a virtual set is only half the way between the simple chroma-key in which cameras were not permitted to perform any kind of movement and the high end systems the industry can offer today in which cameras have complete freedom of movement.

It seems that small stations and production houses should use the 2-D, entry level systems. Given the fact that 2-D systems can always be upgraded, this is not such a bad choice. At the same time high-market stations and production houses will purchase the high end, 3-D systems.

12 Computers in Virtual Studio Systems

The hardware of a virtual studio system is basically an add-on to standard TV equipment. The same cameras and space are used, as well as the same switchers, monitors, recorders and lighting. In a virtual set system the main platform is a computer, sometimes more than one. Existing computer technology at any given moment determines performance of both high-end and entry-level virtual set systems.

In today's high-end systems the most powerful graphic engines are used. Even these, however, leave much to be desired when it comes to rendering of sophisticated 3-D graphics in real-time. The performance of the most powerful graphic engines still does not allow for complex effects such as ray tracing and morphing to be rendered live. Low end systems utilizing low-cost graphic workstations limit the production to use of 2-D graphics, or to offline work.

There are two main requirements from computers used for virtual studio at either level.

1) The computer has to include a digital video I/O card and a powerful graphic-engine.

2) The video I/O card has to be able to handle broadcast quality, 10 bit ITU-R 601 serial digital video (SDI) in NTSC (60 Hz) or PAL (50 Hz), in full broadcast quality according to the standard used in the studio.

Most virtual studio manufacturers install their software on computers purchased by customer from third party vendors. Virtual studio manufacturers provide customers with details of the exact type of computers with all add-ons and accessories to be purchased prior to the installation of the virtual set system.

Almost all manufacturers of virtual studio systems base their products on computers made by the manufacturer that dominates the high-end graphic workstation market SGI® (formerly Silicon Graphics Incorporated). The SGI machines are built to handle 3-D graphics and multiple high definition video (and audio) signals in real time. SGI recognizes the importance and growing potential of the virtual studio industry and is attentive to the special hardware and software needs of virtual studio systems as they are developed.

Most entry level virtual set systems use O2™ computers while high-end systems use Onyx2™ computers. The O2 and Onyx2 are both UNIX® based machines. In entry level virtual set systems a single computer usually does all the work of handling the graphics and the camera tracking system.

Some entry-level or medium-level systems use NT based systems such as Pentium III PCs or Silicon Graphics 320™ or 540™ models. The SGI 540 model is used by Accom's Elset-Live-NT.

Onyx2 Family. Courtesy of SGI.

O2. Courtesy of SGI.

O2 is used as a platform for systems such as ORAD CyberSet-E and the RT-Set Ibis. The O2 can be used for 2-D prerendered virtual sets. It can handle the required movement of the background graphics according to changes of camera orientation and zoom. The O2 can also handle two live video feeds connected to its video interface card. These feeds can be combined in the background graphics. The digital video I/O for the O2 is one of two optional cards available.

The O2 can render only a very limited amount of 3-D graphics in real-time and it cannot perform real-time anti-aliasing making it suitable for offline or 2-D only.

OCTANE. Courtesy of SGI.

In offline there is no limitation to what the O2 can perform, it is only a matter of time. The more complex the set, the more time it will take to render the necessary movement. The O2 features include, 32-bit double-buffered graphics, texture mapping in hardware, Native OpenGL® graphics, hardware anti-aliasing and hardware image mapping support. The O2 also utilizes a dedicated image processing engine as well as video processing and compression hardware.

High-end systems use a powerful graphics workstation such as the Onyx2 and one or two smaller computers to handle camera tracking, animation and various control functions over the main computer. This is done to free the main computer to handle the complex 3-D rendering with no interference. This array of computers is usually connected via an Ethernet network. Camera tracking data is supplied to computers via RS-232 or RS-422 communications.

Onyx2 is used as platform for systems such as Accom Elset-Live, the ORAD CyberSet-O and the RT-Set Larus. The Onyx2 has two different types of graphics engines. The lower level engine is the Reality that can render some 5.5 million polygons per second. The higher is the InfinitReality2, which can render 13.1 million polygons per second. Onyx2 is a multiprocessor machine, supplied with at least two CPUs, which are sufficient for virtual studio needs. The number of processors is not relevant to the ability to render 3-D graphics. This is done by the specialized graphic engine such as the Reality or InfinitReality2 and adding more CPUs will not add power to the graphics engine. The Onyx2, Reality engine, being a high-end, state of the art machine, is expensive and can cost well over $100,000 with all the necessary options. A set of computers for a high-end virtual studio system that includes one Onyx2 with an InfinitRealty2 engine and two O2 machines can cost in the neighborhood of $200,000.

Some manufacturers have developed dedicated computers. These computers are not commercially available and are built to perform a limited number of specific tasks. Such computers are used in pattern recognition and infrared tracking systems for analyzing the video output of a studio camera or an overhead Infrared camera. One such computer is the ORAD DVP 50/100.

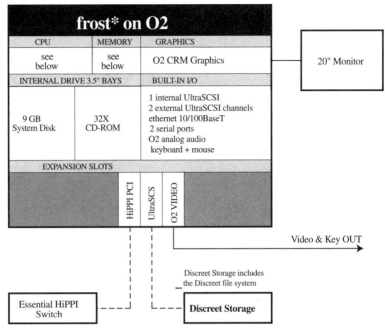

frost* on O2		
CPU	MEMORY	GRAPHICS
see below	see below	O2 CRM Graphics
INTERNAL DRIVE 3.5" BAYS		BUILT-IN I/O
9 GB System Disk	32X CD-ROM	1 internal UltraSCSI 2 external UltraSCSI channels ethernet 10/100BaseT 2 serial ports O2 analog audio keyboard + mouse
EXPANSION SLOTS		

20" Monitor

HiPPI PCI UltraSCS O2 VIDEO

Video & Key OUT →

Discreet Storage includes the Discreet file system

Essential HiPPI Switch

Discreet Storage

specs

configuration

Desktop
Operating system: IRIX 6.5.4f
CPU 1 x R12000 @ 300 MHz, 1 MB secondary cache,
CPU 1 x R10000 @ 250 MHz, 1 MB secondary cache

graphics

Native OpenGL graphics subsystem
Hardware Z-buffer

memory

Minimum 512 MB

audio

O2 built-in stereo analog audio

video i/o

O2 digital video option; dual video ITU-R-601 output (video + key)

Connect a broadcast monitor with 601 serial inputs via the O2's video output, or use an external converter to generate a component analog signal

miscellaneous

9 GB system disk, 2 board slots, optional 3 slot PCI card cage, 1 x 3.5 inch UltraSCSI drive bay , UltraFast/Wide SCSI port, 2 x DB9 serial ports (RS232), 1 parallel port, 10BaseT/ 100BaseT Ethernet, 20" monitor cabling

The diagram illustrates one of many possible configurations.

Courtesy of Discreet.

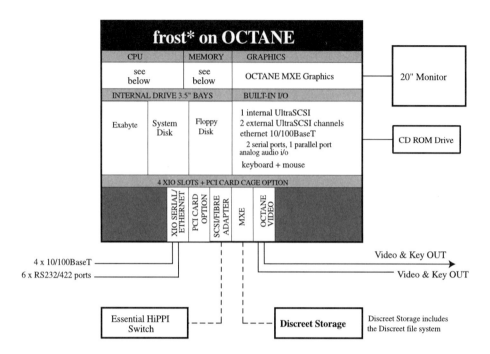

specs

configuration

Desktop
Operating system: IRIX 6.5.4f

CPU 2 x R12000 @ 300 MHz,
2 MB secondary cache,

CPU 2 x R10000 @ 250 MHz,
2 MB secondary cache

graphics

OCTANE MXE

4 MB texture memory

memory

Minimum 512 MB

audio

OCTANE built-in digital AES3/
IEC958 stereo audio

video i/o

OCTANE digital video
option for video I/O;
dual video ITU-R0-601
output (video + key)

miscellaneous

9 GB system disk,
2 board slots,
optional 3 slot PCI
card cage, 1 x 3.5
3 internal SCSI bays,
UltraFast/Wide SCSI
port, 2 x DB9 serial
ports (RS422 and
RS232), 1 parallel port,
10BaseT/100BaseT
Ethernet, 20" monitor,
cabling, Exabyte,
external CD ROM

The diagram illustrates one of many possible configurations.

Courtesy of Discreet.

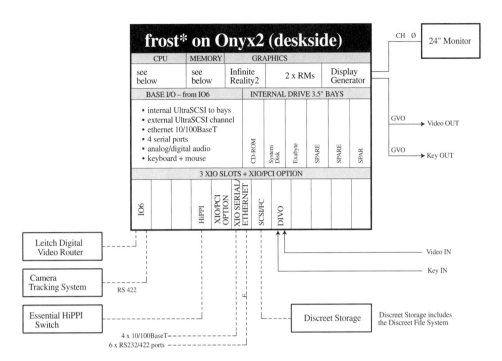

specs

configuration

Onyx2 deskside

Operating system: IRIX 6.5.4f

CPU 4 x R12000 @ 300 MHz, 8 MB cache,

CPU 2 x R12000 @ 300 MHz, 8 MB cache,

CPU 4 x R10000 @ 250 MHz, 4 MB cache,

CPU 2 x R10000 @ 250 MHz, 4 MB cache

Courtesy of Discreet.

graphics

InfiniteReality or InfiniteReality2 with two 64 MB raster managers (RM)

memory

Minimum 512 MB

audio

Onyx2 built-in analog and digital AES audio

video i/o

DIVO dual video ITU-R-601 input (video + key)

GVO dual video ITU-R-601 output (video + key)

miscellaneous

9.1 GB system disk, 5 internal SCSI bays, 4 XIO board slots, optional 3 slot PCI card cage, 4 x DB9 serial ports (RS422 and RS232), 10BaseT/ 100BaseT Ethernet, Exabyte, cabling, 24" monitor

configuration (hdtv)

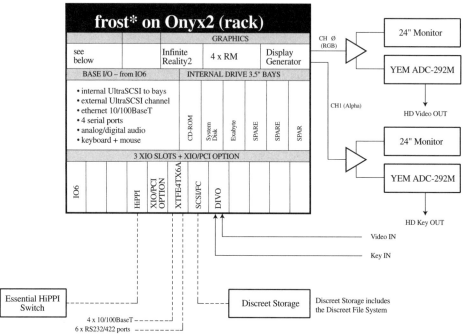

specs

configuration

Onyx2 rack

Operating system: IRIX 6.5.4f

CPU 4 x R12000
@ 300 MHz, 8 MB cache,
CPU 4 x R10000
@ 250 MHz, 4 MB cache

graphics

InfiniteReality or
InfiniteReality2 with
four 64 MB raster
managers (RM)

memory

Minimum 1 GB

1 GB is recommended
for HDTV

audio

Onyx2 built-in analog
& digital AES audio

video i/o

DIVO dual video
ITU-R-601 input
(video + key)

miscellaneous

9.1 GB system disk, 11 internal
SCSI bays, 11 XIO board slots, optional
3 slot PCI card cage, 4 x DB9 serial
ports (RS422 and RS232), 10BaseT/
100BaseT Ethernet, Exabyte, cabling,
24" monitor

supported HDTV equipment

Scan rate converter: Panasonic AJ-UFC1800

A/D Converter: YEM ADC-1125,
ADC-292M

D/A converter: YEM DAC-292M

Parallel-to-Serial converter: YEM
PSP-292M

Courtesy of Discreet.

13 Software in Virtual Studio Work

In virtual studio work several different software products are used in different stages of the production. The process of creating a new set usually starts with a meeting of creative people such as graphic and set designers who need to decide or suggest several options for the design of the set. Once the details of how the set is going to look and the kind of textures and objects to be used are clear, the graphics artist begins to work.

A virtual set can be either a 2-D, flat artwork or a 3-D model. If the virtual studio system is 2-D, It is much easier to build the set. A 2-D flat graphic is created and rendered in the preproduction stage. Picture-manipulation software such as Adobe Photoshop™ can be used to make background graphics. Common graphical file formats (compressed and uncompressed) such as SGI, RGB, TIF, GIF, JPEG, PhotoCD, and Softimage are used to save the artwork. An Alfa image, that can be used to create a depth effect, can be added to the background. The Alfa channel information is fed to the chroma-keyer that treats certain parts in the background as if they are in the foreground by masking. This means that if, according to the foreground camera signal, an actor should appear in those parts of the composed picture, he will be concealed by a part of the background. If this part is a pillar, for example, it will appear as if the pillar is in the foreground partially concealing the actor. In 2-D sets objects can be either in the background or in the foreground of performers in the studio, according to an initial definition. There is no possibility to determine whether the actor is in front of or behind an object according to his position on the studio floor, as is possible in 3-D systems. However the Alfa channel can be switched on and off thereby eliminating the whole foreground/background effect.

Some 2-D systems software allows insertion of two live video windows into the background. The contents of these windows can be animated.

If a 3-D set is to be used, the 3-D graphics are created on a 3-D modeling software. First the 3-D model is built and then textures are added. 3-D modeling software such as 3-D Studio Max, Alias, AutoCAD, Maya, Softimage or Wavefront, is used to create the 3-D model. These are all commercially known and available 3-D modeling software products.

OpenFlight's MultiGen is another software well suited for virtual set design. Originally this software was developed for flight simulators and other areas where rendering of 3-D animation in real-time was needed. Some effects used in popular 3-D modeling software products such as ray tracing and morphing do not lend themselves well to real-time 3-D real-time rendering. These effects require more processing power than current graphic-engines can provide. MultiGen, being intended for real time work, does not support such effects.

After the 3-D model is finished, texture is applied to surfaces in the 3-D model. Textures are created by software such as Adobe-Illustrator, Libraries, Matador, Photoshop and by scanning. When the 3-D file is finished, it is loaded onto the virtual studio system computer via a Loader. A Loader is a software module that converts popular 3-D animation databases into a format that the graphic engine uses, usually OpenGL®. A Loader is usually made to convert from a specific format. There are converters that translate from one 3-D format to another. These can be used to convert the format of the 3-D modeling software to a format that the Loader can use. A Loader developed by Orad enables loading Softimage databases that include morphing. The set that includes the morphing can be rendered live.

How long does it take to build a virtual set? This is a frequently asked question that is not easy to answer. To build a high quality, complex 3-D environment can take 10 to 12 working days, if performed by someone well experienced. A simple set can take some 2 to 3 days, and even less. There are cases where sets were built in a few hours.

If someone is continuously building sets, certain simple objects or building blocks can be saved to be used in other sets in the future. As a library of elements such as pillars, chairs and tables are constructed, they can save a considerable amount of time in later projects. Such a library can also contain items such as textures and logos.

Sometimes the style of a new set is completely different and objects in the library cannot be used as they are and have to be modified, which is still quicker than having to start from scratch.

The computer hardware is usually purchased directly by the end user and the virtual studio system manufacturer installs all the software necessary to operate the system as part of the overall initial system installation.

The computers come with a basic operating system. The operating system installed on the Onyx2 by virtual studio manufacturers is not necessarily the latest. Some older versions such as the Iris version 6.3 are better optimized to

CyberSet Software and Data Flow

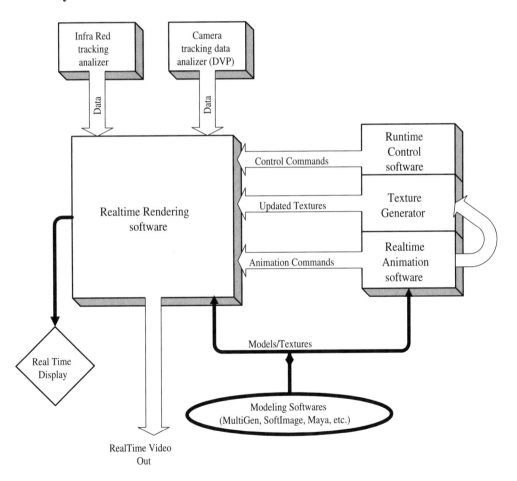

Courtesy of ORAD.

the application. The virtual studio software such as the Orad CyberSet or the RT-Set Larus is installed as well. There is also a software module developed by Silicon Graphics called Performer. The Performer is an intermediate between the application software and the OpenGL. It helps running the application faster and smoother and therefore is very important for the overall performance of the system. Each manufacturer also installs different patches on the computer. Some patches are essential and others interfere with the application software's operation.

Software that operates the video card has to be installed on the Onyx2. Sometimes the software is installed by the computer manufacturer and at other times it has to be installed together with the virtual studio application. In the case of the O2 the video card software comes already installed.

Some manufacturers such as Orad use specially-built computers to perform some of the tasks like picture analysis for pattern recognition and Infrared camera tracking systems. This hardware includes processors and also needs special software to run it. The software has to be reloaded each the time the hardware is turned on. The software is specialized and supplied by virtual studio system manufacturer.

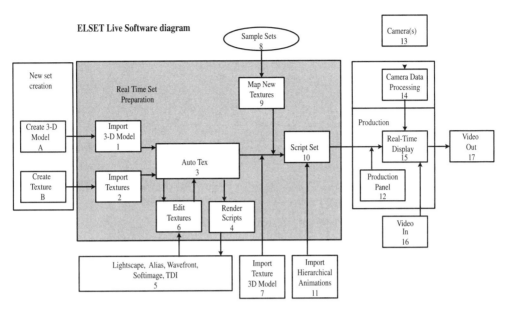

ELSET Live Software diagram

Legend

A. *Create 3-D models*—Alias; Wavefront; Autocad; 3-D Studio MAX; Softimage; Maya.

B. *Create Textures*—Scanning, Adobe Illustrator, Photoshop, Libraries, Matador.

1. *Import 3-D models.* Formats—Inventor; DXF.

2. *Import Textures.* Formats—SGI RGB; FIT; TIFF; GIF; TARGA; PICT.

3 *AutoTex*—Provides functionality for either automatic or manual regrouping of objects, automatic or manual mapping of textures to 3-D objects that constitute the set. Automatic generation of texture rendering scripts. Allows preview of the full set.

4 & 5. *Render Scripts*—The purpose of a render script is to merge lighting information with base textures to enhance the overall realism of a virtual set. Rendering scripts may be created to communicate with the following rendering packages: Lightscape; Maya; Alias; Wavefront; Softimage; 3-DMax

6. *Edit Textures.* Edit functions include—color modifications; cropping, scaling, rotating; edge enhancement; blurring, sharpening; thresholding.

7. *Import of Textured 3-D Model.* Some models built-in any of the modeling packages may be pretextured and ready to run as virtual sets. These sets would not require AutoTex and after conversion to Inventor may be loaded directly into Elset for real-time display.

8 & 9. *Sample Sets and Remapping.* Format—Inventor. Selection of prelit and optimized sets for effec-

tive off-the-shelf use are provided to assist with training or allow for immediate productions. These sets may be easily modified by remapping new textures to provide a different look.

10. *ScriptSet.* Script event (full capability).

11. *Complex Hierarchical Animations*—Complex hierarchical animations may be created in Alias, Maya, or Softimage and directly imported into ScriptSet.

12. *Production Panel*—User defined GUI to assist in the production of a show. Buttons in the production panel are linked to events defined in the event execution script.

13. *Camera Heads and Sensors*—BBC Free *d pattern recognition system; Thoma Walkfinder/Image Tracker; Vinten Vector 70 (Thoma sensors); Radamec (mobile & pedestal); Ultimatte Memory Head; Panther Crane & Dolly; DMC/Xync; Evans & Sutherland; ATM; Hybrid MC.

14. *Camera Data Processing*—Real time input of camera(s) attributes: pan, zoom, tilt, focus. XYZ cameras are supported; Includes a PC to interface; roll.

15. *Real Time Display.* Special effects include—video texture on/off; complex animations; changing textures or geometries; changing Z distance for Distance key.

16. *Video In*—Video in for live textures.

17. *Video Out* – Broadcast quality video outputfrost.

Courtesy of Accom.

frost*, manufactured by Discreet, Canada, is a resolution-independent 3-D graphics system for broadcast production offering real-time external control capabilities and is used for news, financial and sports graphics

frost* workflow

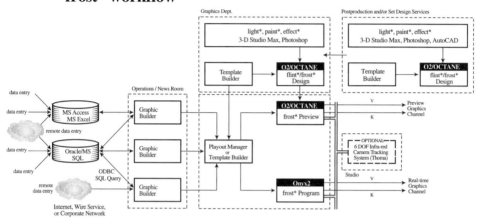

typical workflow, using frost* with producer on-air suite

1. Template Creation

Performed once only (e.g., start of sports season)

Create graphic & animations in frost*

Create Producer templates for each distinct graphic style

Write external control scripts for transitions between various graphic styles

Define transitions between various graphic styles

Configure dynamic data fields for automatic update from live data sources

2. Project Creation

Performed weekly or daily (e.g., weekly magazine show, daily news show)

Select from template library to create new project (e.g., 6 pm news template)

Create individual Producer graphics pages based on template pages (e.g., slug 1, lower third 2, bumper 5, etc.)

Enter story titles, headlines, and other text like standard word processor

3. Playlist Creation

Performed weekly or daily

Put graphics pages into sequential lists for playout in desired order

4. Playout

Load playlist into Playout Manager

Send frost* graphics to air at the touch of a button

Courtesy of Discreet.

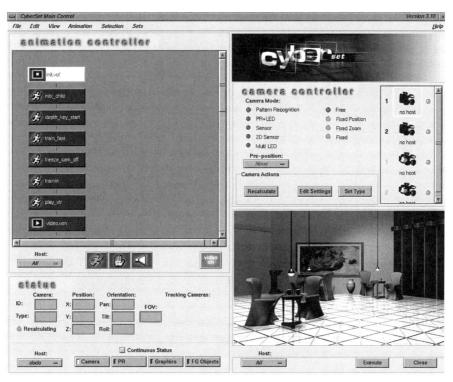

Main control window of CyberSet. Courtesy of ORAD.

Cafe set. Courtesy of ORAD.

14

Video Equipment and Delay Lines

A virtual studio system is computer based and involves very little additional video hardware other than what already exists in a typical TV studio. In some cases switchers or routers are needed to select the particular camera that will be connected to a chroma-keyer. In cases where more than one chroma-keyer is used, a router selects chroma-keyer signals to be sent to camera viewfinders.

If the studio where the virtual studio system is to be installed is an analog environment, analog to digital (A/D) and digital to analog (D/A) converters are needed. Since virtual studio systems are digital, all video signals directly involved must be converted to digital. Usually one A/D converter is needed for each camera in the system. The converters needed are composite or component, depending on the studio format, to 10-bit serial digital (SDI) ITU-R 601. Such converters are common equipment in studios and are available from several manufacturers.

One (or more) D/A converter is needed to convert the system's output back to analog. Again the output should be in whatever format is in use in the studio composite or component. The number of D/A converters needed depends on the number of virtual studio system outputs. In a simple system one output is used and up to three could be needed when a dissolve system with preview is used. In the last case, two converters are used for the two parallel system outputs and one for the preview output. The D/A converter used for the preview channel can be a lower cost, 8-bit unit.

Some virtual studio systems use electromechanical sensor pan and tilt heads. These heads are fitted with sensors that measure the movement in both axes. The camera movement data is delivered in RS-422 format. In such cases the heads of all the cameras involved have to be replaced.

Except for the pattern recognition camera tracking systems, all other systems require electromechanical sensors to measure zoom and focus changes. Such units can be fitted to most common camera lenses. These units also produce data in RS-422 form.

The chroma-keyer is an important link in the virtual studio system. Manufacturers of virtual studios define what kinds of chroma-keyers can be used with the system. The chroma-keyer is usually not supplied with virtual studio systems and is one of the items that has to be purchased by the client. If an existing keyer in the studio is not on the list of required equipment, in most cases another chroma-keyer has to be purchased. The kind usually required is an Ultimatte model 7 or higher. In some systems more than one keyer is needed. For a dissolve arrangement, two high quality keyers are needed. If a preview option is employed, an additional keyer is needed. A keyer used only for preview can be a simple, low cost unit.

The processing of camera tracking information takes time. The more sophisticated systems produce a delay of some two frames. What happens in the system is that the background graphics are rendered according to camera tracking data. The rendering itself is done in real-time. The output from the graphics engine is late by a few frames in reference to the foreground camera video signal. To compensate for the delay in the background rendering, the foreground has to be delayed as well. A video delay line has to be inserted into the video path between the studio camera and the chroma-keyer that combines the foreground and background. The length of the delay needed is equal to the delay produced by the camera tracking system. Manufacturers of virtual studio systems provide information about the delay times in the system. In systems where there is a delay, and the output signal is sent back to camera viewfinders, the picture in the viewfinder will lag behind the actual movement of the camera. This can be annoying and takes some time to get used to.

If the video coming out of the studio is delayed, the audio also has to de delayed. An audio delay line is usually installed in the audio control room on one of the mixing console outputs. The delayed audio is used in virtual studio work as the main audio signal for most purposes. The monitoring to the studio is the only exception. Using delayed audio monitoring in the studio might cause unwanted echo effects and confusion to performers.

15   Camera Movement Tracking

The most important difference between the classic static chroma-key technique, that did not allow movement of the foreground camera and a dynamic virtual studio environment, is the ability to accurately measure the movement of the foreground camera and move the computer-generated background accordingly.

The role of the camera tracking system is to provide the graphic engine accurate and timely data of what exactly is the point of view of the camera. The calculations involved in some camera movement tracking systems require huge amounts of data processing. Every frame of video that comes out of a virtual studio system includes the foreground camera picture composed with the computer generated background after it has been moved in 2-D or 3-D space according to the camera movement.

Most camera movement tracking systems used today for virtual studio work, are new and specially developed. Electromechanical sensors were used previously in robotic camera systems. Several other, nonmechanical systems have been developed since 1995. Most of the new systems impose few limitations on camera work, and perform the task with high precision. Some of the systems work outdoors as well as indoors, and many demonstrate a high degree of ingenuity.

Each camera can move in six different ways (degrees of freedom). It can move its orientation angles: Pan, tilt and roll. It can change its position in 3-D space—x, y, and z; these are all movements of the camera body. Zoom and focus are movements of elements within the camera lens that also affect the camera output image by increasing or decreasing the perceived size of the image. In everyday camera work any number of these movements can be combined.

There is a major difference between systems that measure only the orientation and zoom change of the camera and systems that measure also the position of the camera in 3-D space. In order to effectively use 3-D animation as background for a program, it is essential that the camera move to change the perspective and the viewpoint from where the background is seen—otherwise a flat 2-D background can be used with pretty much the same effect.

Some early or entry-level virtual studio systems can only measure orientation angles and not camera position. This means that the camera cannot move during shooting and cannot be used handheld or mounted on a Steadicam. This limitation decreases the realism and the depth perception of the set.

The camera tracking system has to provide a steady stream of data that has to be synchronized with all other studio systems while providing a reading of the camera position, orientation, zoom, and focus parameters at field rate. The time taken by tracking systems to calculate the parameters is the main reason for using audio and video delay lines in virtual set systems. If, for example, the calculation of parameters takes two frames, the video signal of the camera has to be delayed before reaching the chroma-keyer. Otherwise the background movement will be two frames behind the camera movement. If the stream of data stops during camera movement, the background in the composed output will stop moving. This will cause an unnatural effect and is obviously unacceptable during live transmission.

The following are the requirements of a camera position measurement system sufficient to create good registration. Neither one of the systems can provide all these properties, but some come fairly close:

1) Ability to measure the position of the camera to a degree of precision of no less than 2mm and the orientation to no less than 0.5 pixel. Such orientation precision will mean, for example, that in a long shot 16 degrees wide, a precision of 0.01 of a degree is needed. The narrower the shot, the greater the angular precision needed.

2) Ability to calculate the camera orientation and position, within a very short period of time. In current systems it takes between 8 milliseconds in Electromechanical systems and up to 80 milliseconds in systems such as pattern recognition.

3) The camera tracking system has to calculate and deliver the complete camera orientation and position data at a constant rate of some 60 times per sec-

ond. This is required to follow fast camera movements. If the data delivery rate is insufficient, the background will follow foreground camera movements in a segmented way. The faster the camera movement, the more visible segmentation of the background movement will be.

4) The camera position measurement system should not constrain camera movement in any way. The system has to allow free movement of the camera in any studio or space.

5) The system should not change the way camera operators are used to working. This is especially important where the same cameras and studio are used for virtual studio work as well as standard studio operation.

6) The camera should be allowed to point in all directions, ideally a 360 degree shooting sector.

7) The system should work from any kind of camera mount—standard studio pedestal, robotic pedestal, crane, tripod, and handheld.

8) The system should be able work everywhere, in the studio and outdoors.

9) The system should be able to work with every kind of professional TV camera and impose no limitations on the kind of lens used.

Tracking all camera movements has to be performed with great accuracy. A computer processes tracking data and the background computer-generated image is moved accordingly. The background must accurately follow any kind of movement made by the foreground camera. Sometimes fast and complex movements are made by cameras necessitating in such cases very fast data processing.

Usually several cameras are used in a studio. Camera tracking data stream is switched at the same time with the switching of the video signal from different cameras. If a cut is made in the production switcher from camera 1 to camera 2, the data from the camera heads has to be switched respectively in a parallel router or switcher. The camera tracking data is processed and fed to the graphic engine that moves the background accordingly.

There are several methods of tracking camera movement. Some methods use electromechanical transducers and others employ different kinds of pattern recognition and infrared tracking which require sophisticated software and fast computers. Every method has its pros and cons and no one method has all the advantages. High end, sophisticated virtual studio systems tend to employ two camera tracking systems to ensure that camera tracking data will be available and accurate at all times.

Following is a description of the leading tracking systems in use:

Electromechanical sensors:

These sensors are located on the pan and tilt head around the axes of angular movement and translate every fraction of a degree of movement into electronic pulses. The accuracy of such sensors today can be up to 1,000,000 divisions per 360 degrees of movement. This means that a movement of less than one thousandth of a degree can be detected.

Additional sensors are located on the camera lens to detect zoom and focus changes that affect the image magnification. These lens sensors can be fitted on most camera lenses but not all. The system has no restrictions regarding studio height or size. It allows the camera to pan 360 degrees and can also be used outdoors. Electromechanical sensors that can be attached to lenses as well as pan and tilt heads, are manufactured by Thoma, Radamec and Vinten among others.

Railed tripods or special pedestals fitted with sensors can measure longitudinal movement of the camera mount on the studio floor and/or elevation of the camera. Motion around the studio floor with this kind of sensor is very limited. The same sensors can be used for film cameras.

Electromechanical sensors need a relatively complicated calibration and set-up procedure. Each camera, in the studio, that is part of the virtual set production, has to be fitted with a complete

Sensor, pan and tilt head. Courtesy of ORAD.

set of head and lens sensors. Robotic camera support devices such as pan and tilt heads, pedestals and cranes can also be used as part of camera tracking systems. Since the robotic devices usually get commands from a computer and return data, their orientation and position is known and can be used by the virtual studio system.

The Auxiliary Camera Tracking System:

In this system a small camera is mounted on the main studio camera. The camera is aimed straight up to the studio ceiling. On the ceiling an array of markers is mounted. One version of the system called "Free-d" was developed by the BBC R&D and sold by Radamec under license from the BBC. In this system 8" circular bar-code patterns are used. The bar-code markers are made of a retro-reflective material, which is lit by a circular array of light-emitting diodes mounted on the auxiliary camera.

Four of the ceiling mounted markers have to be seen by the auxiliary camera at all times. The larger the studio, the more markers will have to be mounted on the ceiling. The distance between markers is typically 3 feet in each direction. There are limitations in the size and height of studio to be used in. This system allows the use of different camera mounting systems and also handheld cameras.

A specially built processor calculates the exact orientation and location of the camera.

Electromechanical sensors still have to be mounted on the lens to measure zoom and focus changes. Obviously the ceiling mounted marker system cannot be used outdoors.

The auxiliary camera tracking system allows for an angular shooting sector of some 360 degrees when using ceiling mounted markers.

The Infrared Sensor Camera Tracking System:

ORAD Hi-Tec Systems have developed, and manufacture a system called "InfraTrack." InfraTrack is usually used as a complementary system to the pattern recognition system. This system utilizes an array of four low intensity infrared emitters mounted on top of the studio camera. Several infrared tracking cameras, typically two or four, are mounted on the studio ceiling. The larger the studio, the more cameras will be needed. Each emitter flashes at a specific frequency and has to be seen by at least two infrared cameras. Image processing software recognizes the light source image in the tracking camera frame and calculates its location in frame coordinates. Each frame coordinate is relative to a specific direction relevant to the tracking camera position. The location of the light source image in frame coordinates represents the line of vision between the tracking camera and the light source itself. This correlation is

Camera fitted with part of the InfraTrack system.

calibrated during the system installation. Knowing at least two lines of vision and the relevant tracking camera position in the studio space enables the calculation of the 3-D position of the light emitter itself.

An image-processing unit is supplied with the system that performs the following:

1) Digitizes the infrared tracking camera video.
2) Measures the light source line of vision from each tracking camera.
3) An image processing procedure calibrates the studio camera and the lens's field of view according to the electromechanical sensor data.

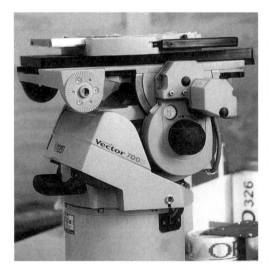 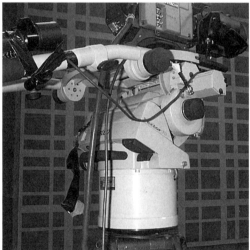

Standard Vinten Pan and Tilt Head equipped with sensors.

A kit of installation and calibration tools is supplied with the system. This set of tools is used to make initial calibration and measurement of the positions of the different components of the system in relation to each other and to the studio space.

The InfraTrack method allows unrestricted camera movement in all directions, and can also be used outdoors. The system requires electromechanical sensors for zoom and focus movement measurement.

Small infrared transmitters can be utilized by the same system to determine position of actors in the studio. The transmitter is attached to the actor's clothes and the system can provide the accurate position of the actor in the studio in 3-D. This attribute is known as depth tracking or depth keying.

Another kind of infrared system, manufactured by Thoma, is named "Wolkfinder". The cameras on the studio ceiling also each contain an infrared emitter. A 3-D array of five infrared reflectors is installed on each camera. The infrared cameras on the studio ceiling detect the reflections and a video signal from the infrared cameras is used calculate camera tracking parameters.

The Pattern Recognition Camera Tracking System:

This is probably the most elegant of all. In the studio there is a special grid drawn on the blue chroma-key background on the studio wall, behind the performers. The grid is drawn in a lighter shade of blue that does not interfere with the chroma-key process. The video signal is fed from the studio camera to a special video processor. Sophisticated software calculates the exact orientation and location of the camera including the zoom and focus settings. All the data needed is extracted from the video signal produced by the studio camera. The system is capable of tracking camera motion according to changes in the image of the grid as produced by the camera. This system can be used outdoors as well. In the case of the ORAD system, data is extracted and processed by specialized hardware called Digital Video Processor (DVP) which is capable of performing an impressive amount of 30 Giga operations per second (DVP 100 model). From the processor, data is streamed in a parallel interface to the graphic engine that renders the background accordingly. At the moment pattern recognition takes longer than other methods to produce camera tracking information—some four frames. A faster system that will be able to do the job within one frame is being developed and will be soon ready. The DVP is used also to perform other tasks not directly related to camera tracking.

This system allows the use of all camera-mounting systems as well as hand-held cameras. Except for the grid on the wall nothing is added or changed in the camera heads or any other camera mounting equipment. Also, there is no need for electromechanical sensors on the lenses. The drawbacks of the system are that the studio camera needs to see at least a part of the grid at all times and the image of the grid has to be focused. In low light conditions this can be a problem. Another problem is that actors can sometimes obscure the grid. The need to see the grid all the time limits the width of the sector that the camera can cover. To solve this problem sometimes grids are located on two or three walls of the studio. Typically the horizontal sector that the camera can cover using a center grid is some 150 degrees.

There is another variation to this kind of system. A small auxiliary camera is mounted on the large studio camera. A two-tone grid can be mounted on the wall of the studio behind the cameras, on the ceiling or in any place where the view is unobstructed. The auxiliary camera is pointed at the grid and is used by the pattern recognition system as the source of data. This arrangement is used when large objects are positioned in front of the cameras in the studio between the cameras and the wall where the grid is located. The pattern recognition method requires no extra hardware on camera heads or lenses. Calibration and set-up procedures are very short, a matter of a few seconds at the most.

Camera Tracking System Comparison Table:

Parameter	Electromechanical	Auxiliary camera	Infrared	Pattern recognition
Independent mechanism to measure zoom and focus	Required	Required	Required	Not required
Close-ups	Not limited	Only limitation is target being obscured. Not a problem	Not limited	Limited by the requirement to capture 2 grid lines in each direction
Mechanical stabilization/ isolation requirements for the studio installation	Eliminate camera roll while moving	Target should be stabilized to few mms. Not a hard requirement	The overhead cameras should be stabilized to 0.01mm. Necessitates special isolation construction	None
Angular shooting sector of the broadcast camera	360 degrees	360 degrees in a ceiling mounted configuration, ~200 degrees for a backwards off-studio target	360 degrees	Limited by the requirement to have a portion of the grid in the field of view. Typically—150 degrees. This limitation is relaxed using a triple configuration
Cost	Expensive. Economy depends on number of studio cameras	Mid-range. Economy depends on number of studio cameras	Expensive. Economy depends on number and motion area of the studio cameras	Very low. Additional studio cameras don't add to the cost
Eye safety problem	No	No	There may be a problem in certain system architectures, especially the retro-reflective configuration	No

Parameter	Electromechanical	Auxiliary camera	Infrared	Pattern recognition
Motion area of the studio cameras	Limited. Strongly depends on the sensor type	Strongly dependent on studio geometry and the system configuration in off studio grid	Limited by the coverage of the overhead cameras	Not limited
Studio logistics, flexibility to switch from a virtual to a normal production	High	Low	Low	High
Calibration and setup procedure	Complicated	Relatively complicated	Relatively complicated	Very simple
Compatibility with low-ceiling studios	Full	Full	In low-ceiling studio the cameras motion zone and/or system accuracy become impractical	Full
Compatibility with studio lights	Full	Major problem especially in a "ceiling viewing" configuration of the auxiliary camera because lights obstruct the target and auxiliary camera is saturated by the lights	A major problem in certain configurations, especially in the retro-reflective method	Full
Support of "mobile panel" (billboard) configuration	No	Yes	No	Yes
Support of a remote configuration (central processing station serving several studios)	Logistically complicated and expensive	Logistically complicated and expensive	Logistically complicated and expensive	Low cost and easy (just foreground video needs to be transmitted)
Support of a "real set" configuration (insertion of virtual elements into real scenarios)	Yes	Yes	Yes	No

Parameter	Electromechanical	Auxiliary camera	Infrared	Pattern recognition
Compatibility with studio camera types	Full support of all types and opera-tion modes	Crane cameras and shoulder mounted opera-tion are not sup-ported in several systems	Does not practi-cally support crane cameras because the receivers do not cover the desired shooting height. Shoulder mounted or handheld oper-ation is not suppor-ted by all systems	Full support of all types and all operation modes
Compatibility with studio camera lenses	Requires an independent mechanism to measure zoom and focus. Possible in most, but not all studio lenses	Requires an independent mechanism to measure zoom and focus. Possible in most, but not all studio lenses	Requires an independent mechanism to measure zoom and focus. Possible in most, but not all studio lenses	Full compatibility with all types
Compatibility with camera's peripheral equipment	Full	A camera moun-ted prompter is usually not sup-ported; not all viewfinders/ monitors types are supported	A camera mounted prompter is usually not supported; not all viewfinders/ monitors types are supported	Full
Processing time delay	1 frame	1–2 frames	1 frame	1–2 frames
Chroma-keying quality, shadow reconstruction capability	No limitation	No limitation. In case of an off "off studio" tar-get, more careful adjustment is required in an in studio configur-ation	No limitation	Good quality and shadow capability is possible but requires more careful adjustment

In addition to the other virtues, of all the above-mentioned camera-tracking systems the pattern recognition is the most cost effective. In budgetary terms it is best suited for entry-level systems, for studios with a relatively large number of cameras and for a number of studios using the same virtual set system.

Choosing the best tracking solution for a specific job is complicated and involves many considerations. It depends on the studio specifications, the kind of camera movement and production requirements.

Since no one tracking system is perfect, a combination of two systems will give better coverage with less errors and more precise camera parameters. Each manufacturer uses different combinations of tracking systems, according to the systems available and to the needs of the specific system. Sensor heads go well with all other tracking systems by providing precise orientation angles.

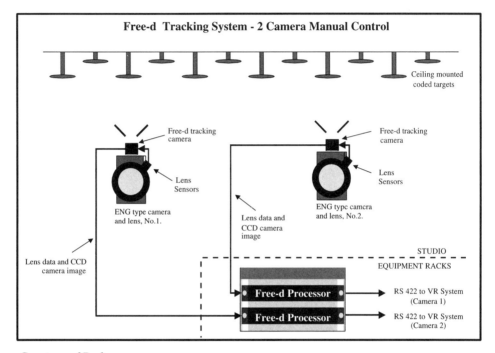

Courtesy of Radamec.

Some entry-level systems such as the Getris Psy, don't use any kind of camera tracking system. Instead, the camera is fixed firmly in place. A kind of DVE movement of the foreground camera picture is performed in the system computer together with some movement of the background. A limited movement of pan, tilt and zoom can be made that looks like camera movement. This way the system can be simpler and lower in cost.

Sometimes robotic pedestals and camera pan and tilt heads are used as part of camera movement tracking systems. When using such systems camera orientation and position are known and this information can be supplied to the computer rendering the background.

Free-d auxiliary camera.

Radamec RP2 VR robotic pedestal.

16 Camera Switching and Dissolving

In a conventional TV studio, switching and dissolving different camera signals during recording or transmission is a routine action done many times in a normal working day. The production switcher that is standard equipment in TV studios executes these actions. However, switching and dissolving in a virtual studio system and every other visual effect that involves more than one camera signal, becomes more complicated and usually requires more equipment.

The ability of a planned virtual studio system to perform on-air switching and other effects between camera signals needs to be carefully planned, since it will largely affect the complexity and price of the system. In some cases it can even double the equipment list.

Basically there are three kinds of systems:

1) A single camera system. This is of course the simplest system with only one camera used and therefore no switching exists. Cameras that are not part of the virtual set system can be used—the problem being that they will not have the same background. Such camera sources can be switched and dissolved with virtual set output but this will usually diminish the affect of the virtual set and therefore is seldom used. This will also introduce video timing problems since the virtual set system output is delayed.

2) A multi-camera system with the ability to cut between any of the cameras. This is the most cost-effective, and therefore the most common configuration.

3) A system with two or more cameras and ability to cut and dissolve between them. This is a high-end, more complex and costly configuration.

A very important part of a multi-camera virtual studio is the preview system. What a camera operator, whose camera is not on-air at a given moment, will see in the viewfinder are performers with the backdrop behind them. If camera one, for example, is on-air, the camera operator will be able to see the composition of his camera's output with the computer-generated background on program color monitors in the studio or in the viewfinder, usually in black and white. The operator of camera two, who is intended to be the next one on-air, has no way of framing his camera in relation to the virtual background. The composition of camera two output signal and the virtual background does not exist yet. Camera position and orientation data has not yet been processed by the system and the background has not been rendered to fit the camera viewpoint.

Additional equipment has to be installed to allow the next camera to be on-air, a preview system that will allow the camera operator, director and others to see the composition before it is put on air.

Because of the added complexity of each camera shot's composition with the computer generated background, the importance of checking the preview before putting it on air is far greater than in a conventional studio production. In principle, to provide a full preview facility a complete additional virtual set system has to be installed in the studio. The input of the system will receive the camera signal to be previewed and the output will be connected to a preview monitor in the control room and to the camera's viewfinder. Data from camera head and lens will be fed to a computer that will render the background according to the camera viewpoint.

The major components in such a system are a computer, a keyer and a router. Since these components will be used for preview only, they can be considerably less expensive than the same components used in the main system for on-air work. The speed of the computer and quality of the keyer are of less importance. A routing system has to be installed to switch camera outputs and serial data signals. As more cameras are added to the systems, more inputs will be needed for the router. The router can be controlled by virtual set system operator or by the production switcher operator in the control room by means of a small control panel.

Most virtual studio systems can handle cut edits with no additional equipment if a preview option is not required. Dissolves between camera signals including the associated computer generated background information, is a much more complex and costly story.

In this case two parallel systems are used. Each consists of a high-end computer and a chroma-keyer. If additional hardware is needed for processing of the camera tracking data (depending on the camera tracking system chosen), that too has to be included. The systems work in parallel and each system processes the signal of one camera with its background. The two outputs are fed to two different inputs of the studio production switcher and can be dissolved with each other. Wipes can also be performed between the two signals. After a dissolve transition has ended, one of the systems is off the air and can be connected to another camera for the next transition.

There is a more complex configuration where on top of the two parallel channels there is a third relatively low cost channel used for preview only.

To ensure very smooth operation every camera can be connected to its own virtual set system. This way every camera operator will see the right background to his shot at all times. In the control room it will be possible to display each camera on a different picture monitor already combined with the computer generated background. This will allow all the professionals in the studio to work in exactly the same way they used to in traditional studio production. Naturally, this is the most expensive setup.

17   Typical Layouts and Block Diagrams

In the following section are diagrams of actual layouts of different systems supplied by the manufacturers. They are intended to provide a better understanding of the possibilities and configurations that are currently available. Each manufacturer can offer different options—only a few are shown here. Systems can usually be customized according to the specific needs and requirements of the customer.

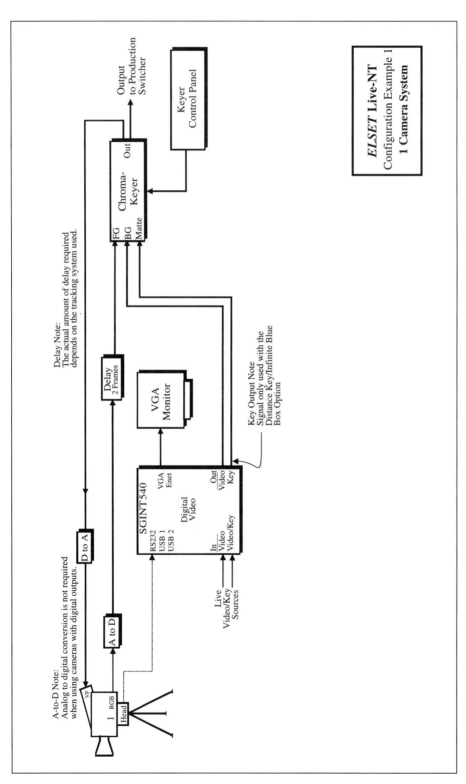

Courtesy of Accom.

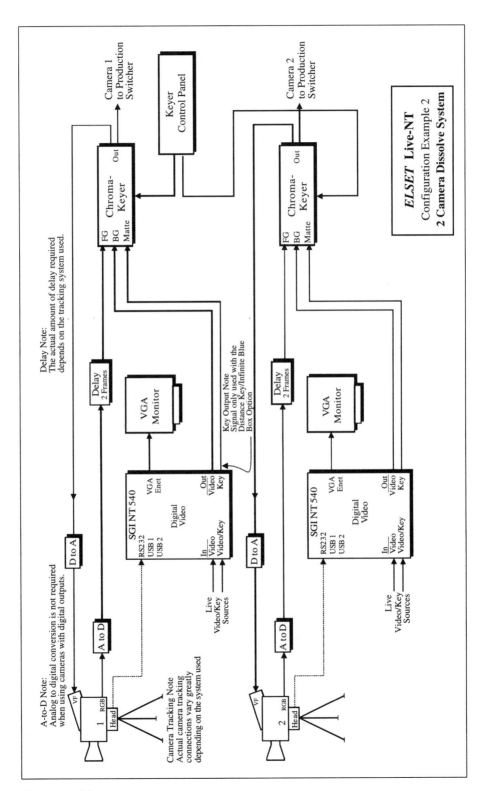

Courtesy of Accom.

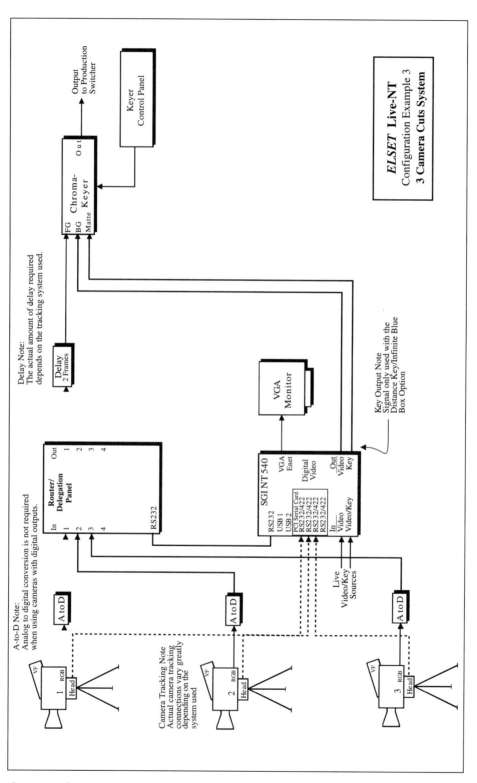

Courtesy of Accom.

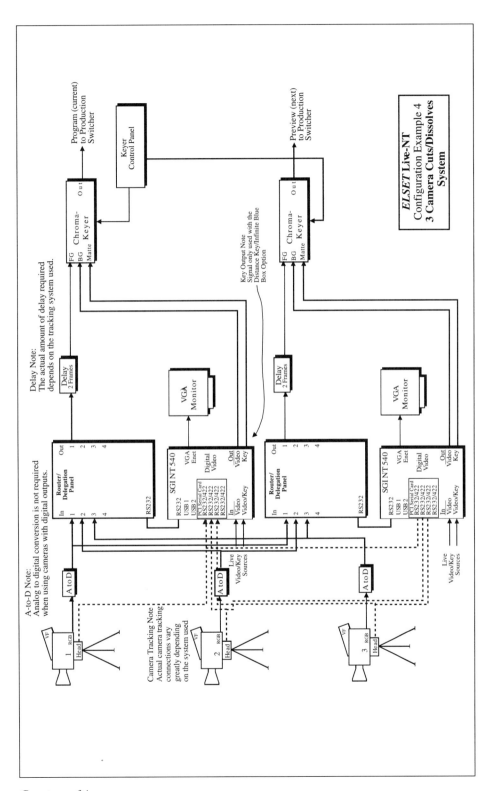

Courtesy of Accom.

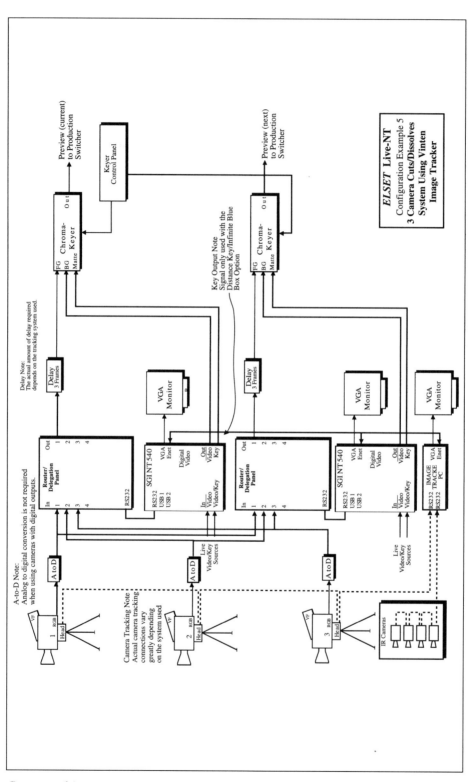

Courtesy of Accom.

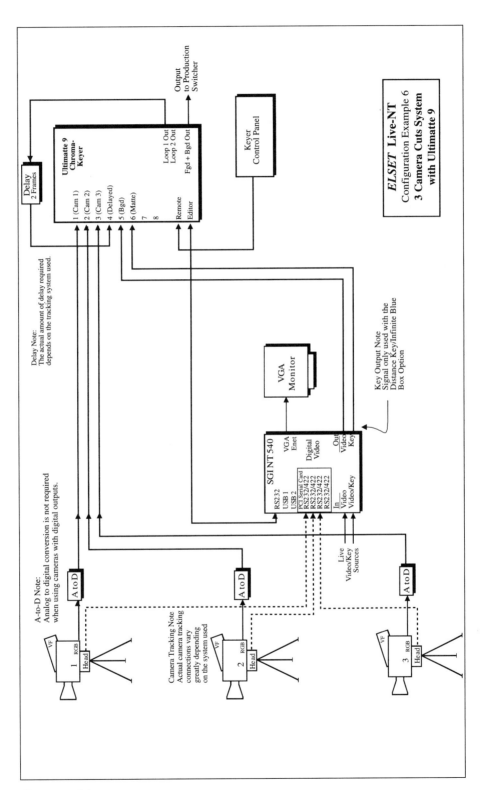

Courtesy of Accom.

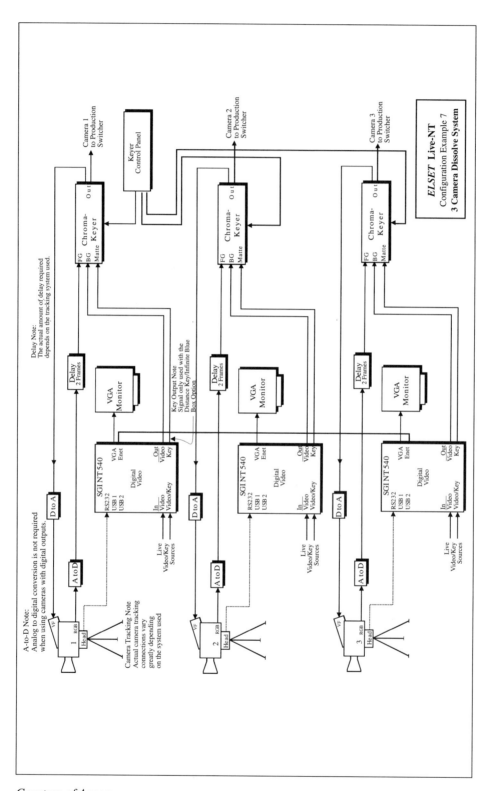

ELSET **Live-NT**
Configuration Example 7
3 Camera Dissolve System

Courtesy of Accom.

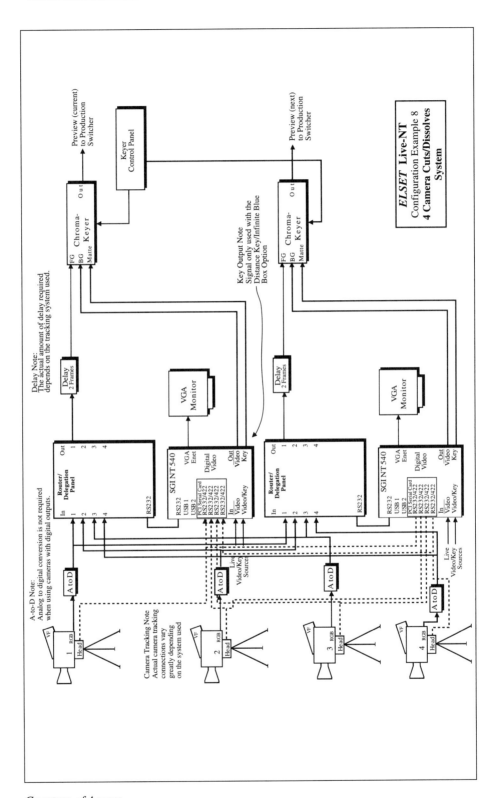

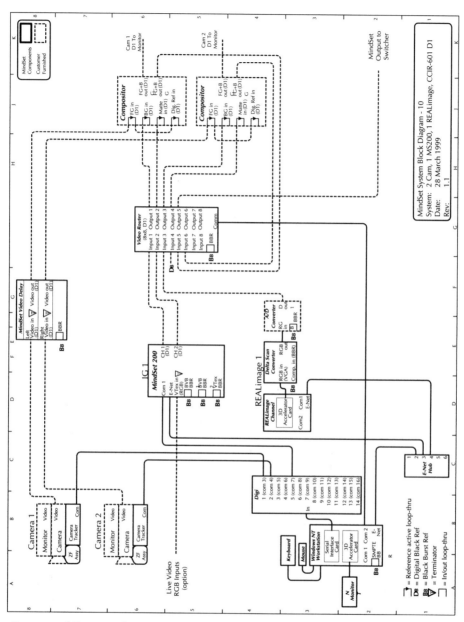

Courtesy of Evans and Sutherland.

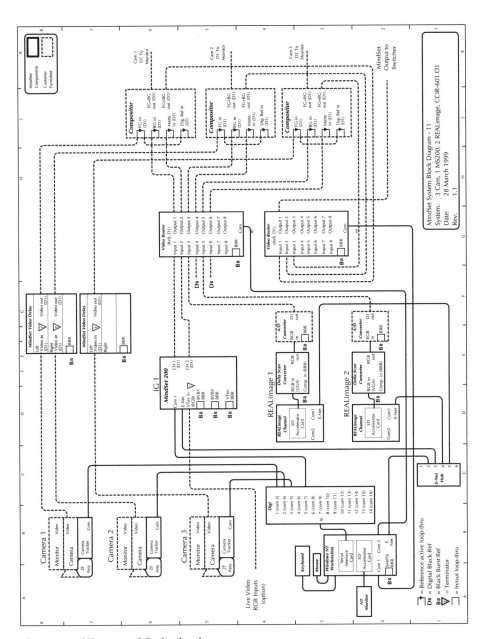

Courtesy of Evans and Sutherland.

MindSet Post™-Remote Acquisition System

Camera 1
Monitor   Video
Camera   Video

ZF   Camera
Assy   Tracker   Com

D/A
Converter
RGB
out
D1   BBR
in   out

D1 Tape Deck
Video   Video out
in (D1)   (D1)

LTC Generator
Time
BB   BBR   Code
out

Time   Time
Code in   Code
BB   BBR   out

VITC Generator
Time
Code in   VITC out
BB   BBR

keyboard

mouse

Windows NT Workstation
Serial
interface
Card

NT
monitor
3-D
Accelerator
Card

Com 1   Com 2
SMPTE   E-
BBR   Net

REALimage 1
REALimage
Channel
3-D
Accelerator
Card

Com 2   Com 1
E-Net

Delta Scan Converter
RGB in   RGB
(VGA)   out
BB
Comp. in BBR

Chroma-Keyer
FG in
(RGB)   FG & BG   Cam 1 to Viewfinder
BG in   out (RGB)   and monitors
(RGB)
BB   BBR

Notes:
1. REALimage channel is optional for viewing composited images.
2. Time code and VITC connections shown are typical and will vary depending on the equipment at the user's site

MindSet
Components

Customer
Furnished

Courtesy of Evans and Sutherland.

MindSet Post Real Time System

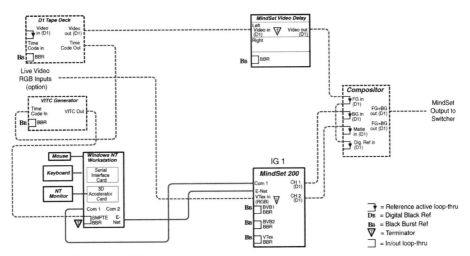

Courtesy of Evans and Sutherland.

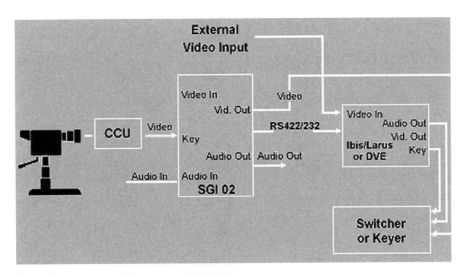

Pica block diagram. Courtesy of RT-SET.

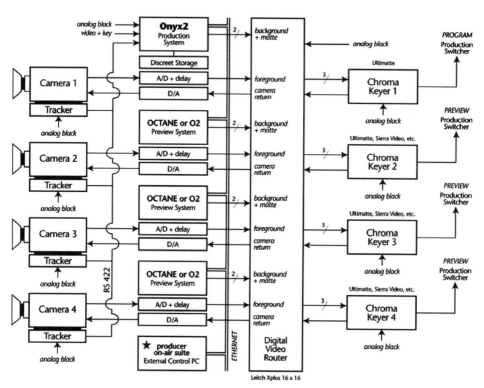

Frost* virtual studio. Courtesy of Discreet.

18 Technical Data Comparison Table

The data in the following tables is based on standardized questionnaires that were sent to the manufacturers of virtual studio systems.

Name of Product	Accom ELSET Post	Accom ELSET Live NT	Accom ELSET Live	Discreet Frost*	Evans & Sutherland MindSet
Level of the system	Low cost high quality	Mid range	High end	High end	High end
Computer used	SGI O2 or higher	SGI Visual Workstation	SGI Onyx Onyx2	SGI Octane or Onyx	Proprietary E&S image generator many configurations
Operating system	UNIX	NT	UNIX	UNIX	NT
Number & type of CPUs	1xR4400 or higher	Intel Pentium III	2xR4400 or higher	R10000 and R12000 2-Octane 4-Onyx	PC dual CPU 1 E&S image generator Windows NT
Recommended amount of RAM	128MB	256MB	256MB	512MB	256MB
Recommended capacity of the hard disk	4GB	4GB	4GB	9GB	9GB
Additional computer hardware needed	No	No	PC		
The graphic engine used	Native GFX of the workstation	Native GFX on Visual Work-station	GFX: Reality-Engine2 InfinitReality InfinitReality2	IR/IR2	E&S Image Generator
Is it a 2-D or 3-D system?	3-D	3-D	3-D	2-D and 3-D	3-D
If 2-D, Can it be upgraded to 3-D?					
The size of back-ground in pixels	Unlimited	4MB, as defined by OpenGL of the machine	IR has 64MB		NTSC/PAL
Can the system record T.C. and camera movement-data for offline work?	Exclusively this way	No	Yes	No	Yes (O)
How many cameras can the system handle live?	1	32 or more limited by serial ports	Unlimited	8	Currently 4— more available
Are additional computers needed?	No	No	PC O2 (O)	Yes, for preview	No
For what purpose is each additional computer			PC—camera tracking, O2—preview option	Preview	
What kind of camera tracking can be used?	Every commercially available system	Every commercially available system	Every commercially available system	Sensor based and infrared tracker	E&S or Radamec any serial based Sensor based (O)
What is the recommended camera system?	Depends on requirements of sysyem	Depends on requirements of sysyem	Depends on requirements of sysyem		E&S

Orad	**Orad**	**Orad**	**Radamec**	**RT-Set**	**RT-Set**
CyberSet E CyberSet Post	**CyberSet M**	**CyberSet O**	**Virtual Scenario**	**Ibis**	**Larus**
Entry level	Mid-range	High end	Entry level	Entry level	High end
SGI O2	SGI Onyx2 RE	SGI Onyx IR	None	O2	Onyx2 IR
UNIX	UNIX	UNIX		UNIX	UNIX
1xR5000	1-(S) 2-(O) R1000/ R12000	2 R1000/ R12000		1 R5000 200MHz	2 R10000
256-512MB	min. 128MB	min. 128MB		256MB	512MB
4.5GB	4.5GB	4.5GB		4GB	4-9GB
DVP (Digital Video Processor)	DVP	DVP			1 x O2 R5000
O2 Graphics	Reality Graphics	InfinitReality Graphics		D1 option for O2	Divo + InfiniteReality
2-D	2-D/3-D	3-D	2-D	2-D	3-D
Yes (O)				Yes	
Up to 4,000 x2,000 (8M)	Depends on many factors	Depends on many factors	Standard video	4K x 4K	
Yes (O)	Yes	Yes	No	Yes	Yes
Unlimited standard is 4	Any number standard is 4	Any number standard is 4	1 per Scenario	Ininite	No hard limit
No	2-3 O2s for animation & tracking	2-3 O2s for animation & tracking	No	O2	O2 per Camera (O)
	1 O2 for animation & control, 1-2 O2 for tracking	1 O2 for animation & control, 1-2 O2 for tracking		Tracking	Preview
Pattern recognition, (S) Sensor based or any other	Pattern recognition, Sensor based infrared tracking or any other	Pattern recognition, or Free-D infrared tracking or any other	Radamec sensor heads	Mechanical	All kinds
Pattern recognition	Pattern recognition	Pattern recognition	Radamec	Hawkeye	Mechanical IR

Name of Product	ELSET Post	ELSET Live NT	ELSET Live	Frost*	MindSet
What is the calibration time needed?	Depends on tracking system, from few minutes to 1/2 an hour	Depends on tracking system from few minutes to 1/2 an hour	Depends on tracking system from few minutes to 1/2 an hour	5 minutes	Less than 30 secs.
Is there a need to add tracking equipment for each additional camera?	Depends on the system. Yes for most systems	Depends on the system. Yes for most systems	Depends on the system. Yes for most systems	Yes	Yes
What kind of additional tracking equipment is needed per camera?	Depends on the tracking system head	Depends on the tracking system	Depends on the tracking system	Full sensor based heads or infrared targets on camera	Tracker per camera
Is a preview channel provided?	N/A	Yes (O)	Yes (O)	No	Yes (O)
What kind of chroma-keyer is used?	Any cheap one for preview	Any, Ultimatte is recommended	Any, Ultimatte is recommended	Ultimatte	User supplied
How long does it take to install the system?	From 1/2 hour to 1/2 day	From 1/2 hour to 1/2 day	From 1/2 hour to 1/2 day	1 day	1/2 day
Can the system work in HDTV environment?	Yes	No	No	Yes	
Can system be upgraded to work in HDTV?		No	No		
Can the system be connected to more than one studio?	Yes	Yes	Yes	Yes	Yes
Live video input option?	No	Yes	Yes	Yes	Yes
Garbage matte option?	Yes	Yes (O)	Yes	Yes	Yes
Depth keying option?	Yes	Yes (O)	Yes (O)	Yes	No
Multiple live video windows?	No	Yes	Yes	Yes	Yes
Depth of focus effect option?	N/A	Yes (O)	Yes (O)	Yes (O) Requires Ultimatte 9	No
Shadow reconstruction on background option?	No	No	No	No	No
Virtual camera function?	Yes	Yes	Yes	Yes	Yes
External scoring and statistics input option?	No	Yes, as live data input API	Yes, as live data input API	Yes	Yes
Audio and video delay management?	N/A	Yes	Yes	Yes	Yes
Audio segment automatic insertion?	N/A	Yes	Yes, (sound option)	Yes	No
Ray tracing?	Yes	Yes	Yes	No	No
3-D text?	Yes, from authoring package	Yes	Yes	Yes	No
Real time motion capture?	Yes	Yes (O)	Yes (O)	No	No

CyberSet E	CyberSet M	CyberSet O	Virtual Scenario	Ibis	Larus
Not needed	Not needed	Not needed	10 minutes during installation	2 to 3 min.	5 min.
Not in pattern recognition	Not in pattern recognition	Not in pattern recognition	Yes	Yes	Yes—Tracker
			A head or Free-D camera	Tracking Head	Tracking Head
Yes (O)	Yes (O)	Yes (O)	N/A	No	Yes
Any digital chroma-keyer	Any digital chroma-keyer	Any digital chroma-keyer	Any kind	Any kind	Any kind
3 to 10 hours	1 to 1.5 days	1 to 1.5 days	1/2 day per camera	1 day	2 to 3 Days
No	Yes	Yes	No	No	Yes
No			No	Yes	
Yes	Yes	Yes	Yes	No	Yes
Yes	Yes	Yes	Yes	Yes. 2, full resolution	Yes. 2, full resolution
Yes	Yes	Yes	No	Yes	Yes
No	Yes	Yes	No	No	No
Yes	Yes	Yes	No	Yes	Yes
No	Yes	Yes	Yes (O)	No	Yes
No	Yes	Yes	No	No	Yes
Yes (O)	Yes	Yes	No	No	Yes
No	Yes, (Can be customized)	Yes, (Can be customized)	No	No	Yes
Yes	Yes	Yes	Yes	No	No
No	Yes	Yes	No	No	Yes
Possible only in postproduction	Possible only in postproduction	Possible only in postproduction	N/A	No	No
No	Yes (O)	Yes (O)	N/A	No	No
No	Yes (O)	Yes (O)	N/A	No	Yes

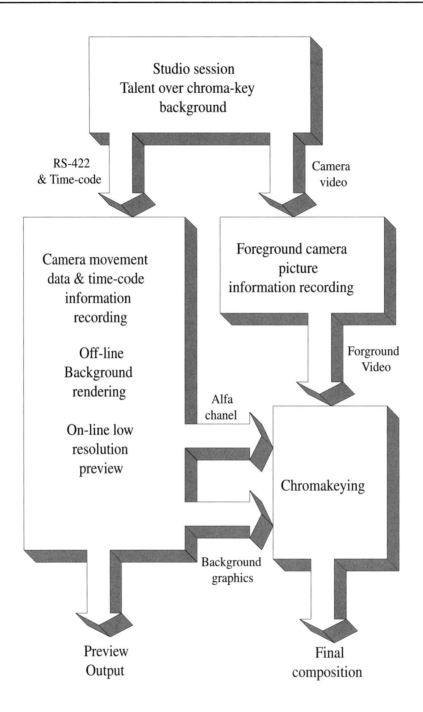

19 Virtual Set in Postproduction Mode

Even though virtual studio systems use high-end graphic engines, the computers used impose certain limitations on rendering complex 3-D graphics in real time in relation to camera movement. These limitations are basically the number of polygons the computer has to render and the amount of pixels to be mapped. Effects such as ray-tracing, texture-mapping and the addition of live video require powerful computing resources. When a program or clip utilizes a very high degree of graphics sophistication, it is not always possible to render the graphics in real-time and the only way to do it is in the postproduction process. This means of course that such programs cannot be transmitted live and have to be prerecorded.

Some systems such as the ORAD CyberSet Post and the Accom ELSET-POST, make it possible. Such systems are capable of operating as a live, real time virtual set and also to render the program one frame at the time. The program is recorded on tape as if it is live. On tape, only the foreground camera picture is recorded. At the same time the system records camera movement parameters, time code, and depth key information can also be recorded. Depth key can be used to indicate the position of actors or performers during the program. A low resolution or wire frame version of the full resolution graphics is used as background. This will be displayed on monitors in control rooms and in the studio as a preview only which is not recorded on the tape at this stage. The preview will allow the production crew and actors to see what the composite signal will look like. It also helps actors in the studio to locate themselves in relation to the 3-D background model. On tape only the foreground camera information will be recorded including the blue or the green background.

Material recorded in the studio can be edited, and segments can be used selectively during the postproduction process. After the program has been recorded, the background graphics are exported to rendering software such as the 3-D Studio Max® or Softimage 3-D®. The background can then be rendered offline, frame by frame, with a full resolution background, and any number of additional effects. The rendering process is made according to the time code signal and camera tracking information recorded in the system. The result of the rendering process is stored in the computer.

The next stage is to composite the foreground video and the background graphics. The videocassette is played and the computer runs the animation. A graphics card in the computer converts the graphic files to video. The two video signals are fed into a chroma-keyer which combines the two signals.

In the postproduction offline virtual set process, complex scenes that cannot be produced even on high-end real time virtual set systems, can be rendered successfully. Postproduction virtual sets are suitable mostly for short items such as video clips, commercials, promos and special effects that require complex graphics. However longer programs can be made as well—it only requires a larger storage area in the rendering computer.

An offline system such as CyberSet Post can use relatively low cost computers such as the Silicon Graphics O2, (as opposed to the Onyx, for example) and at the same time produce highly complex and photorealistic scenes. The same low-cost system can be used for online transmission from the studio, but with less complex background animation.

20 Lighting and CCU for the Virtual Set

Virtual set technology consists of compositing a foreground video camera signal and a background computer-generated image. These two are combined together by a chroma-key process. In order to achieve realism in the resulting composite picture, proper and precise illumination has to be applied to the blue (or green) backdrop and to performers in the studio. Lighting has to be carefully planned in coordination with the graphic designer of the set and preferably also with the chief cameraperson as well as with the technical people such as the camera control person.

In essence, lighting for a virtual set is the same as for any chroma-key situation. However, the extra dimension of camera movement involved in the use of virtual sets, makes lighting more complicated and demanding. Any flaw in the background lighting that under normal conditions would be invisible, will become apparent the moment the camera starts moving.

To avoid problems of camera control, light levels on the blue backdrop and performers should be the same. An incident light measurement taken from the same gray card placed in the key light of the performers and in the illumination of the background should produce exactly the same reading. Chroma-key results will not be improved if the background illumination will be stronger.

Illumination of the performers should not light the background and vice-versa. This is easy to do in a large studio with great depth but requires special attention in small studios. Since the option of using smaller studios while still getting good results is one of the more attractive advantages of the virtual studio, small studios will be used more often thereby giving lighting directors a hard time. Light from the foreground might harm the precise even spread of light on the backdrop. Direct light from the background lights could change the required balance between the performer's key and fill lights. Spill of blue light reflected from the background might cause blue contours around performer's figures and change the color of their back light.

It is recommended to start the lighting setup in the studio with lighting the performers and other foreground elements. The basic lighting of performers is the same as in any classical TV production consisting of key, fill and back lights. The lighting used in the computer-generated background should be noted and the lighting of performers in the studio be set accordingly. Distinct differences in level, softness and hue of illumination might cause performers to become separated from the background in an unnatural way—which can completely ruin the merging of foreground and background we are trying to achieve. If, for example, the background is a bar at night, illuminated with a small amount of soft, reddish light, a performer lit with bright white light will stick out from the background and the whole scene will look odd. Side and backlights of performers are of added importance. The performer will appear with dark edges against a brightly illuminated background if not properly lit.

Most manufacturers of virtual studio systems recommend Ultimatte equipment, model 7 or 8 chroma-keyers for chroma-keying. It is the industry standard of high quality chroma-keying, even though there are other chroma-keyers on the market. Ultimatte recommends a specific color for blue background, which is known as "Ultimatte Blue." This color is used to make the backdrop material and to paint other objects in the studio, which are parts of the blue background. It will give the best results with Ultimatte chroma-keyers.

Set parts placed on the studio floor in various places are used to hide performers in certain places on the set or in places where there are stairs or tables in the background graphics. Blue painted set parts can create lighting problems. The top of such surfaces can be hotter than the floor due to being much closer to studio lights. A darker blue paint can be used for the top of set parts to balance the light to that of the floor. "Gothic Ultra Blue" paint is recommended for that purpose (again, by Ultimatte).

Tops of set parts can also cause glare. Light reflected from surfaces is the same color as the light source, irrespective of the color of the surface. This means that even if the floor is blue, the glare will be white and will cause problems in the chroma-key process. Floors in TV studios, being made from materials with a different texture than the cyclorama, always present problems. The angle at which the light hits the floor is also different. One solution is a change in the position of certain overhead lights. The lights should be moved back towards the camera and tilted up so that the light will come from the direction of the cameras. This will eliminate the glare from the floor but part of the light might hit the cyclorama. Another option is using polarizing filters on cameras. Such filters are very effective in eliminating glare from all surfaces but as always there is a price to pay. Polarizing filters reduce the amount of light entering the camera by two or even two and a half F-stops. In such cases higher levels of light have to be used for the entire studio, foreground and background, thereby creating additional heat which has to be dealt with.

The blue background has to be seamless and very even in color and texture. It is not enough that it will all be the same color since different textures reflect light in different ways. Lighting of the background has to be even in terms of the intensity. Dimmers should not be used to alter the intensity of cyclorama lights or any other lights used to illuminate the blue background. They will cause the color temperature of lights to drop, making the light more yellow. All lights should have the same color temperature. When using dimmers, all dimmer circuits should be correctly adjusted to produce the same output voltage when at maximum power.

The color temperature used does not have to be exactly 3,200°K but it has to be consistent throughout the studio. A good method to check light level on the background is by using a waveform monitor connected to the foreground camera output. If the camera is aimed at the blue background, small variations in brightness will be highly visible, including gradual falloffs from side to side in the background or from top to bottom. This method is more precise than a light spot-meter when it comes to checking for minor light intensity changes over a large area. Connected the same way, a vector-scope can be very helpful in checking if the color temperature of the light is uniform across the background. The dot on the screen that marks the blue parts in the picture should be as small as possible. If it is smeared it means that you have variations in color temperature of lights on the background.

There is a method of using yellow or amber gels for the back light of performers in the studio to eliminate blue spill from the background. This method should not be used where an Ultimatte chroma-keyer is used since they deal with spill differently.

Usually there are problems to properly light corners of the background evenly. Corners and the lower edge of the cyclorama where it meets the floor needs to be covered with specially made round elements. Companies such as "Pro Cyc" make modular cyclorama systems that can be fitted in almost any size of studio. Such systems provide easy installation and a smooth, rounded blue background.

Correct camera white balance is important. The white balance has to be made on a white card placed in the key light of the foreground. It is essential that the color temperature of the light should be exactly the same for the white balance and for the actual taping of the program. If a polarizing filter or any other filter is used during recording (or transmission) of the program, the same filter arrangement has to be used during the white balance process. The white card should be placed in such a way that it will not be affected by bounce light from the blue background or overhead fluorescent auxiliary lighting.

The correct alignment of studio cameras is vital. Gray-scale charts or slides should be used to adjust each camera's red, green and blue channels for white, black and gamma throughout the signal-processing path in the camera. This process requires a great deal of precision and know-how. A minor misadjustment of gamma, for example, in a single camera can cause great changes in camera output color where it matters the most. Such misadjustments can be negligible in normal studio production but in a virtual set situation it can make it impossible to achieve clean chroma-key or cause considerable inconsistency between cameras.

Camera iris should not be fully opened. This will cause darkening in corners of the frame in most camera lenses. It is recommended that the iris be closed to at least one f-stop less than the maximum possible aperture. If there isn't enough light in the studio, boosting the gain on the camera will not do any good and will only add a considerable amount of noise to the video signal, thereby making it harder for the chroma-keyer to operate. If there isn't enough light for the studio cameras, there is no other choice but to add more.

Filters such as diffusion or fog filters are not recommended for use in virtual set production. Such filters smear blue light from the background onto the foreground subject. If a softer look is needed, detail circuits on the camera can be adjusted for less detail. Also a thin black nylon stocking stretched across the front of the lens can be used to make the picture softer.

In conventional chroma-key work mattes are used to cover parts of the frame which are not covered with blue background such as the ceiling. In virtual set production simple mattes cannot be used because of the camera movement. Mattes cannot follow the complex movements that cameras perform. Therefore, matting has become part of the virtual set engine. The same software that moves and renders the background graphics can take into account that certain parts of the background need to be treated as blue at all times.

Perhaps this is the place to describe a new cyclorama lighting system called "Truematte" developed by the BBC Research & Development Department. To resolve most of the problems mentioned before, such as spill, and uneven lighting of the background a new method has been developed. A special material, called "retro reflective," is used for the background. This material consists of tiny glass beads coated on one side with a highly reflective layer that reflects light to the exact direction from which the light comes. Another important property of the retro reflective material is that it is a very efficient reflector. It reflects light several times more than white paper, for example. Retro reflective materials are not new and are used in road signs to increase visibility of the sign at night and in low light conditions. The light from the car headlights hits the sign and comes right back towards the car. Because of the highly reflective qualities of the material, the sign appears to be brightly lit. In the studio the retro reflective material is used instead of the conventional blue or green cyclorama fabric. Another major advantage is that this material, being so reflective, needs a fraction of the illumination usually applied to cyclorama for chroma-key purposes. It is enough to fit a ring of some 40 blue LEDs around the camera lens. The power consumption of the LEDs is 6 watts which, compared to the tens of kilowatts of power usually needed, is negligible. The light from the LEDs is sufficient for the chroma-keyer to recognize the background as blue. The saving in power reduces heat in the studio and saves money in electricity bills and light bulbs for cyclorama lights. When using this method there is so little light on the cyclorama that most spill problems disappear.

To use a green background instead of blue all you have to do in this new system is to change the ring of LEDs on the lens to one with green LEDs. The retro reflective background will work with any color of light. When you look at it in daylight it is gray. The retro reflective material works best when the light hits at right angles to the material. Working in close cooperation with the manufacturer, the BBC improved the qualities of the retro reflective material to reflect light coming from a wider range of angles. Light from the LEDs hits the floor of the studio in normal working conditions at angles of up to 80 degrees from the perpendicular. The improved material is capable of effectively reflecting light back at such flat angles.

According to the BBC there is no longer a need for the lighting director to spend expensive studio time on lighting the cyclorama and dealing with spill problems when the Truematte® lighting system is installed. The Truematte® lighting system has been installed and is working successfully in the BBC's new virtual studio at BBC Television Center in London. This studio is used for the production of a wide variety of programs and also serves as a center for Research & Development.

As can be seen, lighting for virtual sets is a complex and demanding art, but lighting was never easy. It is possible that in a few years time lighting will become easier and less time consuming thanks to developments such as the retro reflective materials.

The work of the lighting director in a virtual studio environment can be somewhat disappointing, since the effort in lighting a virtual set goes mostly to satisfy technical needs and systems. If the lighting director does a good job, it will help the combination of performers and computer-generated background to look convincing. In conventional television, the job of creating a certain mood or atmosphere is the more enjoyable part of the lighting director's work. In virtual studio projects the set designer and artists create much of the atmosphere.

21 Chroma-Key

The magic of the virtual studio is heavily based on the chroma-key process. Chroma-key which is also known as blue-screen is as old as color television, and much older in cinema. In the early days of television when it was still black and white only, a predecessor of the chroma-key was used, the luminance key.

Both techniques are based on the same idea; a specific component is removed from the picture and another one is added to form a picture composed of two different sources. In luminance-key, as the name implies, parts of the picture which are the most bright or the most dark can be taken out and replaced by other background material. In the chroma-key process a specific color is used as the key to determine which parts of the picture will be taken out. The chroma-key method is in principle more complex than the luminance key. To determine which parts of the picture are to be taken out, more than one component of each pixel has to be checked. The three components of the video picture—luminance, chrominance and hue—have to comply with the predetermined levels and phases.

The blue color is used most of the time as background for chroma-key. Sometimes green is used as well. In principle any pure color can be used, but there are different considerations that made the blue color the most commonly used. The primary reason is that blue is the complementary or the opposite of skin tone. Since most of the time people are in the foreground, it is easier to differentiate between the skin tone and the blue background. Another advantage of blue background is that blue reflections from the background (spill) onto talent in the front are better dealt with than reflections in other colors. Green background has an advantage in that cameras are more sensitive to green than to other colors and also the green channel in cameras has the most detail. However, green spill is very noticeable, more so than others and also it has been found that it is more pleasant for people to work in a "blue box" than in a "green box."

Chroma-key has been used for many years now in television in a variety of ways. It is used to combine two pictures that are otherwise impractical or impossible to join together. Sometimes a set is too large to fit in a studio or too expensive to build. Only a small part can be built in the studio and the rest can be made as a drawing that will be combined with the real part by a chroma-key effect.

The most common kind of chroma-key effect is where the background of an announcer or performer in the studio is replaced by another background. If the chroma-key is properly done, a convincing illusion that the performer belongs in the artificial background can be obtained. Usually an actor or announcer is placed in the studio with a blue (or green) background behind him. The blue parts in the picture are then replaced by another background picture from a different source such as a still picture placed before another camera in the studio, graphics or video coming from a videotape recorder. Meteorological maps or pictures of clouds can be placed behind a weather person, news events as they come in through the satellite can be placed behind a news announcer and a background of hand painted graphics can be placed behind a group of dancers or a singer. Naturally, still objects can be placed in the foreground as well as people. The possibilities of composition with chroma-key are endless.

The instrument that performs the actual chroma-key process is the chroma-keyer. The chroma-keyer can be part of the vision-mixer in the studio or it can be a separate unit. In multilayer vision-mixers there is usually a chroma-keyer for each layer. There are two kinds of chroma-keyers, a nonlinear and a linear type. The first one to be used was the nonlinear or switching keyer. Two video sources are connected to each keyer and one video signal comes out. The keyer has to combine the incoming sources according to keying parameters. The early keyers used to switch between foreground and background during the scanning of each frame. Where there was blue in the foreground, the background was switched to the output and where there was no blue, foreground was switched to the output. These were the only two possibilities, however, the switching method presented some problems. In places in the frame where fine detail existed such as presenter's hair against the blue background, switching between foreground and background along each scan line had to be performed very quickly. Such quick switches were not always available. Inadequate switching speed causes loss of fine detail in the output picture.

With switching or nonlinear chroma-keyers there is another limitation with transparent or translucent objects and with smoke. Transparency means that you need to see some of the foreground and some of the background, through the foreground object. Such a mix is not possible with a nonlinear chroma-keyer. It will switch either to the foreground or to the background. The result will be poor and unconvincing.

Then came the linear keyer. The linear chroma-keyer can mix together foreground and background information in proportions determined by the amount of blue color of each and every pixel of the foreground picture. Every proportion of mix can be obtained from full foreground to full background.

Shadows cast on the backdrop and on the floor are another problem. Sophisticated linear keyers can deal with limited amounts of shadows to create a convincing effect. Usually in areas where the background needs to come into the frame, it comes in full color and brightness. In places where there are shadows in the foreground, the luminance of the background has to be suppressed to create the impression of a shadow.

22   Depth Tracking

In an ordinary studio production, performers move freely in the studio and since they act within real scenery, the cameras convey the information of where the performer is in relation to real objects like a table or a pillar. If a performer walks behind a pillar, it is obvious that he will be hidden by it. The performer can move naturally between parts of the scenery just as he walks in his own living room. In a virtual set, things are not that simple. Imagine the following—an elections results presentation. An announcer is moving around in a studio with no scenery. There is only a blue backdrop and a blue floor. Except for the cameras, all the rest of the studio is empty. The virtual studio system replaces the blue background with a 3-D artwork of a set with objects such as scoreboards, video-walls that pop up out of the floor and an elevator that comes down from the ceiling. How can you know the exact correlation between the announcer's position and movement and the position of 3-D objects such as a scoreboard? How can you avoid "collisions" in the combined environment of the announcer in the foreground and objects in the virtual 3-D background?

You can mark certain places on the studio floor with blue gaffer-tape. Usually a picture monitor is placed in the studio where the announcer can see it. The announcer will see on the picture monitor the output of the virtual studio system. This way he will be able to relate to the background, and get some sense of location in the set. But the problem is how will the virtual studio system know where the announcer is? This is where depth tracking becomes important.

We can give the scene a more natural look by allowing the announcer to sometimes move behind some of the objects in the virtual set. What we need first of all is the ability of the 3-D software to define an object (in this case a scoreboard) as either a background or a foreground object according to need. Now we need to know the position of the announcer, whether he is "in front of" or "behind" the object.

Looking through the control room window and switching the definition of the object manually at the right moment could do the trick. A more precise and elegant way, is to put an infrared LED on the announcer's belt and let the infrared camera tracking system determine the exact position of the announcer on the studio floor. The computer that renders the 3-D background receives the information and switches the 3-D object to be background or foreground in relation to the position of the announcer in the studio. If it is defined as foreground at a particular moment, the announcer can be concealed by it. Furthermore, the infrared tracking system can provide highly accurate information regarding the whereabouts of the announcer. This information makes it possible to place the announcer in 3-D space not only before or behind an object but also inside objects such as a small elevator.

In some publications, depth tracking is also called depth keying. Depth tracking is gradually becoming an essential part of virtual studio systems as they become more sophisticated and often employ more than one method of camera tracking each of which complements the other—such as pattern recognition and infrared tracking. The infrared tracking system can be used for depth tracking with a relatively small addition of equipment.

In the area of depth tracking there is an interesting development. An Israeli company named 3DV Systems Ltd. has developed a product named ZCAM™, which is described in more detail in Chapter 31.

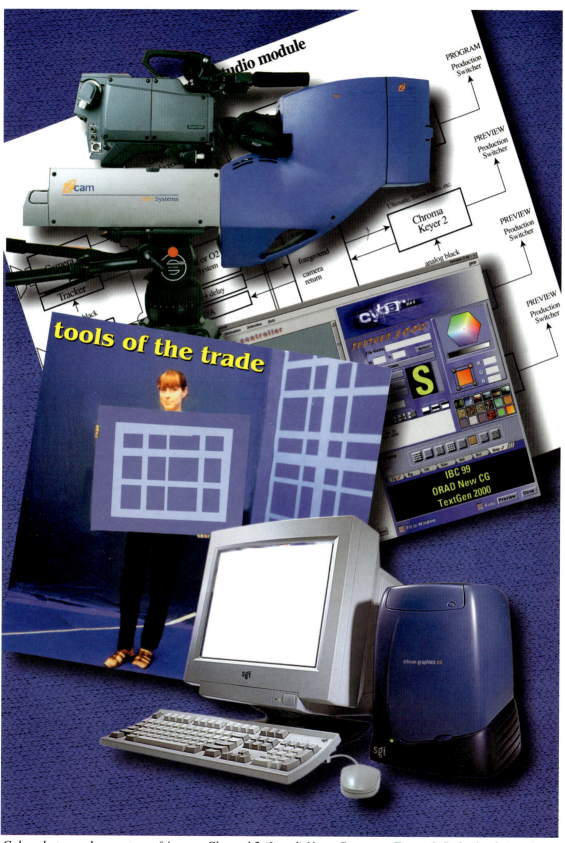

Color photographs courtesy of Accom, Channel 2 (Israel) News Company, Evans & Sutherland, Israel Broadcasting Authority, Nitrofilm, ORAD, RT-Set, SGI, Sky Sports, TV-Frankfurt, and 3DV Systems.

from photo-realistic to surrealistic

23   Calibration and Registration

These terms are frequently used in relation to virtual studio systems. They also have different meanings in other fields. Both terms refer to the relationship between 3-D real and virtual spaces and viewpoints. The real studio is a 3-D space. The virtual set is also a 3-D space. In the studio there are several cameras each with a different viewpoint of that 3-D space. In the computer there is a virtual camera or viewpoint from which the virtual set is seen. Calibration and registration are about the procedures that link these two 3-D worlds together and link viewpoints to spaces.

If we analyze the viewpoint of a camera in order to define it, we will find that we need to know eight different parameters. These parameters are divided into several groups. There are six degrees of freedom—pan, tilt and roll are the orientation angles, X, Y, and Z define the position of the camera. Zoom and focus change the camera picture by magnifying it. All these parameters have to be measured for each camera in the studio continuously, at field rate.

The parameters are sent to the graphics engine that runs the 3-D background. The graphics engine moves the virtual background to be seen from the same orientation and position of one of the real cameras in the studio, one that is "on-air." It is not enough that the computer receives a continues stream of camera tracking data, it needs also a known reference point to which it can relate. The procedure of passing this information to the computer is called calibration.

The calibration procedure is performed as follows: cameras are located at a specific spot on the studio floor, pointed towards a special target positioned in a specific place on one of the studio walls. The zoom and focus controls are fixed at specific settings. While the cameras are pointing at the target, the tracking system performs nullification. From that moment on, even if cameras move the system will know the exact orientation of each camera in relation to the studio space. If cameras change orientation, sensors in the camera heads and lenses will transmit data that will allow the tracking system to know what changes have been made.

Entry level virtual studio systems use 2-D artwork as background and the cameras in the studio cannot move from place. Since the position of cameras is fixed, the calibration procedure defines only orientation, zoom and focus data. The calibration procedure described here is done for electromechanical sensor heads, infrared sensors and auxiliary camera tracking systems. Such calibration is a time consuming procedure and can take up to half an hour. A pattern recognition system can determine within a fraction of a second all the necessary initial parameters just by analyzing the image of the grid in the video signal coming from the camera.

Registration is a procedure in which the computer that generates the 2-D or 3-D background is correlated with the picture of the foreground cameras. Registration can also be defined as the equivalence between viewpoints. The viewpoint of the real studio camera and the viewpoint of the virtual camera in the computer. If, for example, a news announcer has to appear in the composite output as if he is behind a desk. He will sit in the studio behind a blue box with the same proportions of the virtual desk. In the background drawing or animation will be the desk that will eventually be seen in the composite output. However, adjustments have to be made to assure that the announcer in the studio will appear exactly in place, behind the desk in the background. These adjustments are referred to as registration. From the moment the registration is completed, the background will be locked to the camera picture, and follow any movement the camera makes to maintain that correlation.

One of the advantages of virtual studio is that the set can be several times larger than the studio space. This presents a certain problem when correlating between the two. In the planning stage of the virtual background this problem has to be dealt with. A portion of the virtual set has to be defined as the active part of the set. This part matches the size of the real studio, and only in this part will you be able to see the combined output of the system, performers or real objects in the studio. All the rest of the virtual background will be used only to enhance the feeling of depth and opulence. After the registration procedure has been made, the viewpoint of the real and virtual cameras will be matched and linked together.

In some systems there is a possibility to use a virtual camera to capture areas of the background that are beyond the limits of the real studio cameras. Such virtual camera shots can be combined with real camera shots. Absolute and highly precise calibration and registration are essential between the real video picture and a graphic model to achieve convincing results. The calibration and registration have to be maintained throughout the recording or transmission. Loss of any of these adjustments will cause the actors or announcers to lose their position in relation to the background. It can, for example, cause the news announcer to float in the air above his desk. This is, of course, not something we want under normal circumstances.

Audio block diagram

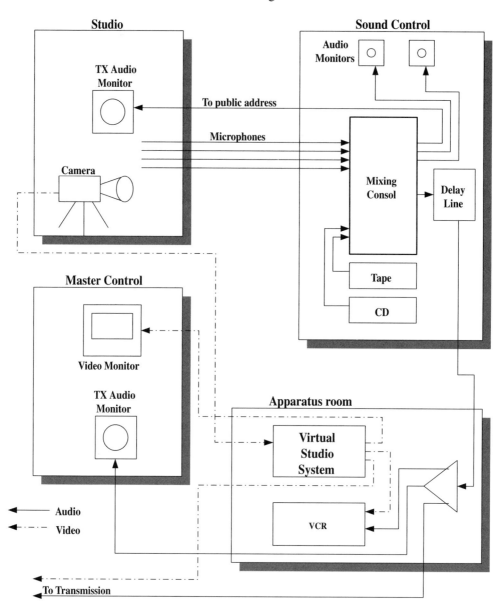

24 Audio in the Virtual Studio

Television is composed of vision and sound that travel from the television studio through the production, postproduction and distribution stages to the television set in the viewer's home. The debate, which is more important, vision or sound, will probably never be settled. Sound can easily exist without vision in forms such as radio while video without sound will take us back to the days of silent movies.

It seems that at this stage of the evolution of virtual studio technology not enough thought went into development of audio for virtual studio. Enormous efforts are being made to make the picture richer and more attractive to the viewer. In audio engineering for television however, there are no innovations that can be directly associated with the development of virtual studio technology.

In time probably more attention will be given to the audio part of virtual studio. Perhaps surround sound techniques are the most suitable to go with virtual studio vision, since it gives a sensation of direction and depth, much like moving in a 3-D space of a virtual set animation. This will undoubtedly add extra complexity to virtual studio production. Until that happens, sound for a virtual studio production is essentially the same as for a conventional TV production.

Camera tracking systems produce a delay of up to four TV frames in the virtual set systems. The length of the delay depends on the kind of camera tracking system used. The more sophisticated the camera tracking system is, the longer the delay will be.

The same delay that takes place in the video path has to be applied to the corresponding audio signal. An audio delay line has to be connected at the output of the audio console.

Monitoring audio can introduce some minor problems. Usually the main picture monitor in the audio control room is connected to the studio's main video output, which is already delayed. The audio monitors in the audio control should be connected to the delayed audio signal so that the sound engineer will be able to check at all times that there are no timing differences between sound and vision.

Audio sent to monitors in the studio, if an audience is present, should not be delayed because it might cause an echo. It could also cause some confusion to performers in the studio if they hear a delay in the audio monitoring.

Some virtual studio systems such as ORAD's CyberSet-O can have an optional audio/video management module. This module controls the amount of delay applied to audio channels in a way that will consistently match the video delay. Sound effects can be added to the system and played in predefined points during the background animation motion. This is the best way to ensure precise queuing of sound effects during a virtual set production.

25   Installation and Distributed Systems

Virtual studio systems are built to be part of an existing standard TV studio. This approach saves money and makes installation much easier. Usually when buying a virtual studio system, the manufacturer supplies all the specialized equipment such as camera tracking hardware and various software modules. In some cases the system includes specialized signal processing hardware.

The buyer needs to supply equipment according to a list specified by the manufacturer. The list usually includes the graphic computers, a chroma-keyer or in some configurations more than one, and a simple switcher or router for selecting the camera signal that will go into the system and than on-air. All that has to be supplied and ready in the studio when the installation begins.

In cases where the studio equipment is analog, A/D and D/A converters are needed to supply the virtual studio system with digital signals and convert the system output back to analog.

Manufacturers of virtual studio systems rely on the buyer to have standard TV cameras, a production switcher, monitoring equipment and all the usual TV studio equipment and layout. The studio must have a cyclorama and lighting system suitable for chroma-key work.

Installation of virtual studio system includes the following stages:

1) Installation of hardware in racks: The hardware includes computers, monitors, A/D and D/A converters, video switchers, video delay lines, specialized signal processing equipment and chroma-keyers.

2) Installation of hardware in control rooms: including computer monitors, keyboards and remote control panels of video routers and chroma-keyers.

3) Installation of camera tracking components in the studio: Depending of the camera tracking system used, tracking heads have to replace standard pan and tilt heads. Zoom and focus sensors have to be fitted on camera lenses. Infrared cameras have to be installed in the studio ceiling. Infrared emitters or reflectors are installed on studio cameras.

4) Wiring of the system: The different components of the system have to be interconnected. Video wiring includes connection of feeds from cameras and converters, connection of a video reference signal to the graphic engine computer, wiring of delay lines between camera outputs and keyers, connection of the system output to one of the production switcher inputs, and monitoring connections.

Electromechanical camera motion sensing equipment is connected via RS-232 or RS-422 wiring to computers. Some systems employ a dissolve option. In such cases there are two parallel sub-systems and each includes a separate router, graphic-engine and chroma-keyer. The two parallel channels are connected to two inputs of the production switcher, and separate preview monitors.

If there is more than one computer in the system, they will be interconnected by an Ethernet network.

In some systems audio effects are played from a computer and an audio feed has to be connected from the audio board in the computer to the audio-mixing console. An audio delay unit needs to be connected to delay the studio output.

5) Software installation: This includes installation of user interfaces and setup modules, rendering and visualization modules, plug-ins and various optional modules onto the system computers.

6) Initial setup and calibration: This includes mostly components of camera tracking systems. Adjustment of mechanical components and infrared cameras, setup of camera tracking software.

7) System testing: System functions, timing and integration with the rest of the studio equipment is checked.

8) Training: Manufacturer's engineers provide training to studio staff regarding the operation of the virtual studio system.

It is recommended that the buyer receive, some weeks prior to installation from the system manufacturer, diagrams of the system layout and wiring. Planning ahead of the installation will save time and produce better results. Included in the planning process are the locations of hardware such as monitors, keyboards and control panels in racks, in control rooms and desks and wiring paths.

Manufacturer's engineers usually install all the equipment within a day or two. A good practice will be to provide one week for the complete process of installation, adjustment, testing and training.

A single virtual set system can be connected to more than one studio. It can be used much more economically if it serves several studios. This means that the system is distributed between different parts of a building or facility. The studio space and cameras will be in a different location than the computers that process data from the tracking system and render the system output picture. The system can also be farther distributed between distant locations and have extensions in different cities or even continents. Naturally one system cannot serve more than one studio at same time, but it can be used as part of different studios, at different hours or days.

Many TV stations and facilities houses operate several studios. In such facilities there is usually a central apparatus room, to which all studios are connected. This is an ideal location to install the hardware of a virtual set system.

Routing switchers that handle all signals in a station can also handle the inputs and outputs to the virtual set system. The number of video feeds connected from each studio to the system depends on various factors. If there is a single camera in a small studio such as a presentation studio, only one video line is needed. If multiple cameras are used, the number of video lines depends on the structure of the system.

Camera tracking information RS-422 serial data lines have to be routed from the studio and cameras involved to the virtual set system. When pattern recognition camera tracking is used, the tracking information is included in the camera video signals and no additional wiring is needed. However, a special pattern recognition grid needs to be installed in each studio. If other camera tracking systems are used such as electromechanical or infrared, each studio has to be equipped with tracking heads or infrared tracking equipment.

In cases where the system has to serve several studios, wiring is more complicated, and the installation process might take longer. If the system is relatively complex, and includes functions such as dissolve and preview, it does not make a distributed system much more complicated since the amount of wiring from each studio to the system is almost the same. The added complexity is mainly in the central part of the system, in the apparatus room.

An indication of the creative possibilities that are limited only by the imagination and abilities of the graphic designer. Courtesy of Evans and Sutherland.

26 Role of the Graphic Designer

The work of a graphic designer in a virtual studio production is of vital importance to the program. It is also completely different from graphics made in television until the advent of the virtual studio. In a conventional studio production the scenery, props and lighting determine the appearance of the program. The style, atmosphere and "look" of the program in a virtual set are all inherent in the graphic design. The graphic design and execution of the virtual scenery or environment are at the heart of virtual studio technology. All the great advantages and sophistication of the virtual set technology come to life with good graphics.

A virtual set design can be made in any style. It can look as realistic as an ordinary classroom or office, or it can look like something taken from the palace of Louis XIV. The set can be made in surrealistic style, it can be made to look like a scene from futuristic science fiction and it can also be taken from a Middle Ages horror tale.

The set can be composed of small items blown-up—such as a journey into the human heart or quite the opposite, a journey into the solar system where a lecturer in the studio can float in space within the system to do the explaining. Objects in the virtual set can be defined as background or foreground. The meaning is that a person moving in the studio can appear to be hidden behind objects in the set or blocking them, when seen from the point of view of the camera.

A small studio can become anything one desires, restricted only by imagination and creative ability. For the price needed to build a small conventional news hard set, graphic designers can make a virtual set that will look many times bigger than the size of the actual studio. Such a set can consist of several floors, balconies, a working elevator and several presentation areas for subjects such as local news, foreign affairs, economy, and weather.

A virtual set can easily be modified while keeping its main characteristics the same. Elements such as logos, scoreboards and live video displays can be added or moved around. Characteristics such as lighting and color can be changed at very little cost, and without having to climb ladders to adjust the studio lighting or having people repaint parts of the scenery.

The job of the graphic designer requires a great deal of innovation, creativity and imagination. A virtual environment allows the graphic artist who creates it almost complete creative freedom. Virtual scenery is actually a 2-D or 3-D computer-generated image. There are different levels of sophistication and movements within these images.

A simple background image can be a still image that looks like an ordinary living room. The still image can also look like something nonexistent, completely imaginary. It can be combined of ordinary and imaginary objects. The level of sophistication increases when movement is added.

Dynamism can be applied to the set by using movement of different parts of the set such as walls, displays, floors, elevators and furniture. Insertion of moving elements such as live video sources, animations and scoreboards also contribute to the feeling of movement. Naturally the dynamics in the set have to conform to the content of the program. Too much action in the background can distract the viewer from the content of the program, and become the main issue. If the program is longer than a few minutes, subtle motion and action in the background can add vitality to the program.

One has to take into consideration that movement in the virtual background image is related to what happens in the studio in terms of movement or non-movement of performers and cameras. All that has to be carefully planned. Insufficient planning of the different movements and timing of movements can cause collisions between live actors and virtual set elements. Of course, these collisions will exist only in the output picture of the studio and not on the studio floor.

The designer has to bear in mind that every camera movement will cause the background to move accordingly. If the camera that covers a singer for example zooms out, the virtual studio computers will detect that movement and will cause the background to zoom out as well. If the camera pans left, the background will be moved to the right. All is done to create the perfect illusion that the background is real and that the image coming from the camera and the computer-generated image are one entity. This means that the designer has to plan the background in a way that it will have margins large enough so that when the camera moves horizontally, vertically or zooms, it will not run out of background. The same goes for any combination of movements or changes in camera position. In any case, the camera operators need to know the limits in which they have to work. Rehearsal is essential to reach the degree of coordination the studio crew and performers need to perform the necessary movements as directed.

In a virtual set the laws of nature and gravity don't have to be obeyed any more. Elements of scenery as well as people can be suspended in mid-air and move through "solid" walls. Scoreboards or huge TV screens can suddenly emerge from the floor and a brick wall can become transparent. Naturally it all has to be designed according to the required application. It would not be advisable to make a news announcer fly in mid-air or do anything unnatural. On the other hand, a character in a fairy tale can benefit from such antics.

The design of the virtual set includes also the planning of items placed on the studio floor such as stages, walls and stairs. A wooden wall painted blue can be used to hide performers in certain places on the studio floor. Blue stairs in the studio can be used where there are imaginary stairs in the background and a performer in studio has to go up or down.

Since no real scenery is used, the graphic designer creates the complete environment. Set elements such as walls, stairs, furniture and props can all be created paying attention to the smallest detail as part of the graphic design. The design also takes over most of the creative parts of lighting.

The graphic design of the virtual set requires careful study, taking into consideration all aspects and stages of the program. Proper design of a virtual set requires several questions to be answered:

- What kind of a program is it going to be?
- Is it going to be a children's entertainment program or a serious talk-show or a sports coverage program?
- Is it going to be a one-time program or a series?
- What kind of atmosphere or mood is requested?
- What kind of lighting effects will produce the wanted mood?
- How many sections or presentation corners are needed in the set?
- How many people are going to be in the studio, on-camera at the same time?
- In what way are they going to be located—sitting on chairs or moving around, dancing perhaps?

- Do we want a quiet and relaxed program or a dynamic, full of movement kind of show?
- How many cameras are used in the studio and for what kinds of shots?
- What kind of static displays such as still pictures or logos need to be integrated into the set?
- What kind of dynamic displays such as TV screens, video walls or scoreboards need to be in the set?
- Is 3-D background animation needed or will a 2-D drawing be sufficient?
- Is the program going to be taped of transmitted in real-time or is it going to be rendered offline?
- If a 2-D graphics is planned as background, what are the limitations of the computer that renders the background in real time in terms of the number of pixels, vertically and horizontally?
- Is the 3-D animation going to be prerendered, rendered online or postrendered?
- If 3-D animation is to be used in real time, what are the limitations of the computer that renders the background in terms of the number of polygons?
- How well can the computer handle texture mapping and live video as part as the set?

Once these questions are addressed, the graphic designer can start planning how the virtual environment should look and behave.

When the graphic designer begins creating the virtual environment in which the program takes place, he has to work in close contact with other members of the production crew. Obviously the set design has to be approved by decision makers such as the executive producer and the director of the program. For the decision-making purpose a drawing or storyboard can give an indication of what the set is going to look like and how it is going to function but here the advantages of computer-aided design become apparent, since the designer can show a simulation on screen to vividly bring to life ideas that are difficult to show on a 2-D storyboard. Once the design has been agreed upon, an assessment of facilities and working hours needed to perform the job have to be made to be sure that they are within the boundaries of the budget and available equipment. Sometimes the director comes with his own ideas about how the set should look and perform. In this case the graphic designer's job is to advise the director about the feasibility of the ideas, to suggest improvements and to implement the ideas after a concept has been decided upon.

The next stage is to implement the actual background graphic drawings on a graphic workstation, in full detail, color and resolution. Background can be a 2-D drawing or a 3-D animation, all according to the needs and budget of the program. Most of the time a 3-D background is preferred because it offers more possibilities such as interaction of the talent in the studio with virtual objects.

The graphic designer has to be familiar with the limitations of the virtual studio system in use. Despite the fact that high-end supercomputers such as the Silicon-Graphics Onyx 2 are used in virtual studio systems for rendering of the changes in background in real-time, systems still have limitations. For example, live video sources can replace textures in a 3-D background. However these video sources take a lot of rendering power to be manipulated in 3-D and in real-time. In such cases sometimes the number of polygons in background animation has to be reduced.

Virtual set graphic engines work in one of the following basic modes:

2D—a graphic still image is used as background to action in the studio. The background is moved in real-time according to foreground camera movement.

Prerendered 3-D—all rendering and movement in the background image is made before the recording in the studio. Usually used in low level systems. Allows for a very high scene complexity. Pace of action in the studio is dictated by the pre-prepared background.

Real-time 3-D—Background is rendered live according to unrestricted camera movement. Limits the complexity of the background that can be used. This is the main mode of operation in high-end systems where powerful graphic engines are used.

Postrendered 3-D—During production, camera movement information and time code are recorded and a wire-frame or low resolution model is used for background. The full resolution background is rendered and integrated with the foreground frame by frame in postproduction. Extremely complex backgrounds can be used, mainly for short segments such as commercials, promos, video clips and special effects.

At least one virtual studio systems supplier offers a library of hundreds of virtual set designs to his customers. The designs can be a source for ideas and can be modified to suit different needs.

The graphic designer has to provide the lighting director with the information of what parts of the studio he has to light, apart from the blue background. He has to understand exactly what kinds of movement the performers in the studio will make and which way they will be heading at every stage. Closer to the recording date the chief cameraperson in the studio has to know what the virtual set is going to look like and how it relates to what is going to happen on the studio floor. The same applies to the floor manager and sound engineers.

The graphic designer should be able to quickly respond to changes and growth within the organization as well as changing production needs of the program. Sets can be changed and items can be added faster and more cheaply than the same changes in real, hard sets. A library of set designs made previously for other projects can be stored and readily modified to create new sets.

Some companies that deal regularly with graphics and animation can execute the ideas of the program's graphic designer, and provide the finished file on a CD, optical disk or data cassette. The file can also be sent via the Internet. Finished files can then be loaded into the virtual studio system and be used as background. This solution is suitable for companies or stations that have no graphic workstations or experienced talent to perform such tasks.

In cases where the job of making graphic files has been given to an external company the program's graphic designer has to oversee and coordinate the work. This has to be done with all the above mentioned considerations in mind.

Finally, the look and dynamics of the virtual set is crucial to the success of the program. The creation of virtual sets is a stimulating job in an innovative area where there are not as many rules as in other, more traditional graphic work.

27 Professionals in the Virtual Studio

In a traditional TV studio, scenery elements such as stages, walls, pillars and furniture are real and can be seen by everyone on the set. This is not the case where virtual studio techniques are used.

The work of the different professionals who operate the virtual studio environment is different from that in a studio with conventional scenery. However, it is not a situation that an experienced professional such as a director or floor-manager will not be able to master.

The scriptwriter will have the freedom to write plots that take place in imaginary, fictitious worlds. The director on the other hand, will encounter some problems. When the shooting of a new scene in a new set starts, it will take longer than usual to locate the performers in the studio in relation to the virtual scenery. There is a slight problem with the size and location of actors in the frame in relation to the background, which takes some time to get used to. More planning time and rehearsals will be needed. Movement of performers in the studio must also be more carefully planned and rehearsed.

The camera operators will also encounter some difficulties in accurately framing their shots—especially when making camera movements. Here an external feed of program or preview to the camera viewfinder is essential.

Normally part of the floor-manager's work is to guide performers, guests and interviewees around the studio. He shows them how and when to come in and where to stand or sit.

It is natural for an interviewee to come into a studio set that looks like a living room and sit in a chair opposite the host. In a virtual set all the interviewee will see is an empty space painted blue. There may be a few other elements such as boxes or walls also painted with the same blue color. This can be very disconcerting, especially to the inexperienced. The floor manager has the pleasure of dealing with the confusion of those who come into the studio for an interview or to perform, and find it empty.

The floor manager has to know exactly where each person is to be located, how exactly each performer, announcer or guest should enter and move. Except for the elements of movement, virtual studio work is in fact very similar to ordinary chroma-key.

There might be a difficulty in the communication between crew members. People sitting in control rooms such as the director see on picture monitors the combined output picture of the system. They can say to the floor manager something like "please move the guest closer to the balcony." However, in the studio there is no balcony. The image of the balcony together with the rest of the computer-generated scenery, are combined with the image from the studio. The outcome of the combination can be seen only on picture monitors and not live in the studio.

The floor manager has to convey the instructions of the director to the studio floor while doing the interpretation between the virtual and real worlds. One solution for such situations is the use of large picture monitors in the studio. Several monitors should be placed in different places. The floor manager should be able to see one of them at all times. The host, presenter or performer needs to be able to see such a monitor from everywhere in the studio. The picture monitors should be large enough to be seen from a distance.

The use of picture monitors is not new in TV studios, but in the case of virtual sets it becomes more essential, since in a virtual set the studio space is mostly empty of furniture and scenery, the performers have no reference points to guide them regarding their positions.

The old method of marking things on the studio floor with tape becomes very helpful to talent in virtual sets. If the floor manager marks exactly where the talent should stand and walk, less confusion and mistakes will take place during recording or transmission of the program.

Rehearsal is another routine that becomes even more important when virtual sets are involved. On top of the usual elements rehearsed such as text and movement, there is the element of the "missing" set that causes confusion.

Since virtual studio technology is based on chroma-key techniques, it is very helpful if the studio crew is well experienced in chroma-key studio work. Virtual set productions, being new to most TV professionals, still involve some trial and error in the production stage. The floor manager and producer have an important part in keeping the timetable of the production going as scheduled.

Because of the complexity of virtual studio production most of the programs during the early years used only a few participants. With time the number of participants increases which makes the floor manager's work more difficult.

Talent's view of a virtual studio.

28   Virtual Panels

The virtual panel or virtual billboard is a very handy tool for use in TV studios as well as in the field. The virtual panel is a lightweight flat panel or board, painted with chroma-key blue or green. It comes in any size between 20 cm and a few meters. The panel can be fixed, mobile or handheld and moved freely around by a presenter, reporter or weatherperson in the studio or out. The panel can be used in a virtual set or any other ordinary studio.

Any kind of image such as live video, 2-D or 3-D computer graphics can be displayed on the panel. The panel can be used to display weather charts and maps, news clips, video clips, satellite feeds and sponsorship messages. The panel displays full resolution video at all times. It is an excellent substitute for shooting physical video screens in the studio. No degradation of the image is apparent when the camera zooms in on the panel. The panel can be freely moved and rotated in every direction and angle—the displayed image always follows accurately.

Courtesy of ORAD.

A virtual panel can be a stand-alone system or it can be an add-on to a larger virtual studio system. The virtual panel software runs on a Silicon Graphics O2 R5000.

Video signal from the studio camera is fed to the computer. Position and orientation data for the panel are extracted from the studio by Pattern Recognition algorithms. The position information is fed either to a larger virtual studio system or to a digital video effects unit.

ORAD's Virtual Panel—using pattern-recognition.

ORAD produces a product called MobileSet that can be a stand-alone transportable system or it can be an add-on option for CyberSet E/M/O. On the ORAD virtual panel a grid is drawn on a chroma-key blue background with a lighter shade of blue. The MobileSet system utilizes the same software and hardware components as the CyberSet E. MobileSet was used for the first time at the Soccer World Cup in France in 1998. TV Globo (Brazil), TV Azteca (Mexico), and Caracol TV (Columbia) used it then.

RT-SET produces a product called Pica that can be a stand-alone transportable system or it can be an add-on option for the Ibis or Larus systems. The Pica virtual billboard in its stand-alone version is connected to an effects generator in the studio that receives data from the O2 computer in RS-422 format and an external video signal to be displayed on the panel. Video and key outputs from an effects unit are fed to a switcher or keyer that superimposes the panel on the studio camera picture (also connected to the switcher or keyer).

The virtual panel or billboard is a mini version of larger virtual studio systems. It makes use of the same architecture and hardware components as the larger systems.

29   Advanced Virtual Studio Utilization

One of the reasons that make virtual set systems relatively easy to install is that the amount of wiring into the system and out is small. The initial setup at the beginning of a recording or transmission is also short. These attributes make it a flexible tool that can be utilized very efficiently. One virtual studio system can be used to perform several jobs.

During a production, one set can be replaced by another within seconds. All the expensive studio time needed to change scenery and lighting in ordinary studio work can be eliminated. By a click of a mouse the set can be changed to the same set with different lighting such as day and night, different locations for different scenes of the same program such as office and coffee shop or a completely different set for a different production.

Different programs can be recorded in the same studio using the same blue box, with a swift change of set performed by the virtual studio system operator in the control room. During the time taken for one group of program participants to leave the studio and another group to come in, the new set will be ready. In this way, a studio can be used with very little unproductive time.

Obviously, all graphic files of sets have to be prepared beforehand. It will also save time if the places in the studio of real objects such as furniture and of performers are checked and marked on the studio floor in advance.

Several virtual set systems can be installed in a single studio and each produce a different virtual scene. For example, a large news or weather service provider, can have a single announcer in the studio present a newscast to three different stations each with a different set, different look and different logos in the background all at the same time. Such an arrangement would require only one camera tracking system connected in parallel to all three graphic engine computers. Prices of today's entry level systems make them affordable to almost any professional broadcast facility.

Another way in which virtual studio system's efficiency can be increased is when a system located in a station or building with several ordinary TV studios is connected to several or all of the studios. This arrangement requires wiring the studios to the system and installation of some switching equipment to route the connection to and from each studio. This kind of connection can be planned and performed by any experienced broadcast engineer but it is recommended to consult the system vendor. This method of operation requires adding some equipment to each studio, depending on the kind of camera tracking system used and on the number of cameras.

Pattern recognition is the camera tracking system that is best suited for a multistudio arrangement. Since this system extracts all the camera movement data from the camera video signal, there is no need to connect data wiring such as RS-422 from each studio to the system computer. Usually in a facility with several studios, there is a central apparatus room to which all the signals in the facility are connected with video signal cables. This is the place to locate the virtual set system.

The key to success in such methods of operation is a high degree of planning at several levels. The best way to install and utilize virtual studio systems efficiently starts with consulting several manufacturers and learning what the latest innovations in the field are. Needs and expectations together with the structure of the existing facility should be clear to the manufacturers approached. Based on that information each manufacturer can provide an informed proposal to achieve the goals of the project. Each manufacturer can probably produce more than one proposal at different price and performance levels.

If possible, it would be advisable to send a "delegation" of a few professionals from different areas such as artistic, operational and technical to visit users of systems you consider purchasing.

After the system has been purchased and installed, the station manager has to plan ahead the activities of the different studios in regard to the timetable of the virtual studio system. The availability of the system has to be checked together with the availability of a blue box in the studio. If in the same studio a program has been recorded with an ordinary set, it might take hours to clear the set to the storage area and prepare the appropriate lighting for the cyclorama.

Usually not all professionals in the station or facility such as directors, lighting designers, engineers and camera operators have experience with virtual studio work. The timetable of professionals has to be planned in a way that each function in a virtual set production will be fulfilled with someone with at least some experience. Training of inexperienced staff during virtual studio production has to be planned as well.

If a "central" virtual studio system is used for several studios, routing of camera signals from the studio to be used at a certain time and back has to be performed by engineers at the right time.

Production and floor managers have to be aware of the facility's timetable. Background graphics have to be ready for use, placed where the main graphics engine of the system is and tested.

Courtesy of ORAD & Sky Sport.

30   Virtual Advertising

Virtual advertising is closely related to virtual studio. It is not used in the studio and it's not about sets, but it takes parts of the background of a TV program and replaces them with computer graphics, which is exactly what virtual studio does.

Virtual advertising is a system used in sports coverage of events such as soccer, ice hockey, basketball, tennis, and car racing. It can also be used in any other sports or entertainment event, indoor or out. The system is used for two main purposes.

The first is to replace existing advertising billboards. A virtual advertising system allows replacement of all billboards in an arena with another, carrying the same advertisement in another language or a completely different advertisement. The system can be installed anywhere along the signal path, which means that it can be placed in the outside broadcast truck, back in the station or in another remote station where the signal is received via satellite.

One of the benefits of virtual advertising is that it can put advertisements in places not usually available to be used for advertising thereby increasing the amount of billboards placed in a single sports event.

More than one system can be used to put different advertisements on the same signal. Different advertisements or messages can be targeted to a variety of audiences, in different areas or countries. In multilateral sports broadcasting this could be an interesting way to increase revenues from advertising.

The displayed advertisements or other information can be changed many times during a single game. This means that many different sets of advertisements can be displayed in the place of a single advertising lineup in the arena. Last minute changes are easily implemented allowing online space merchandising and increased revenues. The inserted advertisements can be customized to fit the needs of target audiences in the countries receiving the sports transmission.

The second use of virtual advertising is to insert advertisements or logos in places such as the wooden floor of a basket ball arena, the surface of the water in a swimming pool, or the clay of a tennis court. In such cases the inserted logo is blended in color and texture with the background. Logos and other graphics can also be inserted in empty places above the spectators and even on the spectators in a long shot. Logos can be flat or 3-D live animation.

Courtesy of ORAD and Sky Sport.

The virtual advertising system can be used to place giant virtual video-walls around the field showing additional live camera views, statistics and any external video input. Obviously it will be visible only to viewers at home, not to spectators in the stadium.

Courtesy of ORAD and Sky Sport.

Different informational graphics can be added to the field such as a first down line in American Football and a 9-meter circle around the ball to mark a free kick zone in Soccer. In track and field events different lines and markings on the field can show significant events such as personal or current world records. Virtual advertising systems can also create a virtual runner that runs along with a real runner, at the exact speed of the world record. It can also mark a specific player or the ball by circle that will follow them on the field.

The principle of operation is that the system "learns" the look of the places where advertising has to be placed. During a transmission of a game, whenever any camera, from any angle displays such a place in the arena, the system will identify the right location and replace or insert new information in the picture. At the initial setup of the system prior to the start of the transmission, cameras are pointed at places where billboards are and the system memorizes their exact position.

The ORAD Imagdine system is based on a parallel computer specially built for video processing. It is able to make virtual signs appear via a fade-in or a variety of other ways including a mechanical rolling effect. Each display or change of billboards or other graphics can be prescheduled. It takes some 200 ms to process the incoming video and add the graphical information to frames. Other virtual advertising systems can produce delays of up to 800 ms.

A virtual advertising system needs to cope with several difficult technical problems:

- A large number of cameras is usually used to cover sports events. The system should cope with frequent switching between cameras each having a different viewpoint.
- Cuts between cameras must be followed in real time and the system has to display the right information for each camera.
- The inserted information has to follow cameras that perform fast pan, tilt and zoom motions during the coverage of a game.
- The billboards and other surfaces are often obscured by players. In such cases the graphics of the virtual advertisements should not cover the players.
- Sometimes a player wears clothes of the same color as the background. If a logo is inserted onto a green grass surface, and a player with a green outfit walks on the grass, the logo should not cover him or his outfit in any way. All that while the player is moving in the field and the background is moving in the frame because of the camera movement.

The system should be functional in any kind of weather, light conditions and kinds of arena or court.

Available virtual advertising systems such as the ORAD's Imagdine cope successfully with the above mentioned problems. The virtual billboards are accurately positioned in place in the field or arena. The number of cameras and messages is unlimited. Movement of cameras is followed, and obscuring by players is handled well. TV viewers are not able to tell whether the billboards they see in the arena are real or virtual. Naturally if a huge logo appears on the grass in the middle of a soccer game, viewers might suspect that it is not an inherent part of the grass.

31 What Holds the Future?

To foresee the future is not one of my talents, however, from talking to manufacturers and experts in the virtual studio and adjacent fields, some predictions can be made, with a fair amount of confidence.

If you ask those who produce virtual studio systems what they would like to see improved, the first thing you will hear is faster, stronger graphic engines, with more rendering power. This is at the moment the limiting factor that prevents the virtual studio industry from doing wonders. It is up to the large computer manufacturers to develop faster computers. It is likely that new players will enter the field of high-end graphic engines with strong video capabilities. With improvement of graphic engines, we will probably witness more use of photo-realistic sets that look like familiar surroundings, in more detail and realism than possible today.

Some manufacturers try to harness the graphic rendering power available in high-end virtual studio systems to do additional jobs such as video effects and generation of characters. I believe that we will see virtual studio systems that will take over the functions of several traditional items of equipment such as still-stores, effect generators and character generators. This will allow the production of special effects and graphics in a more sophisticated way. For example, 3-D characters will be able to float in 3-D space of the set, having textures taken from the still store in the same system, and performing 3-D movements. This will also make the complete package of studio equipment smaller in size, easier to install, less expensive and easy to operate.

The delays introduced by camera tracking systems will soon disappear, making the audio and video delay-lines in current systems unnecessary and the systems easier to install.

There is a trend today to use operating systems other than UNIX. This is in an attempt to use cheaper computers and reduce the overall system price. Some manufacturers already offer NT based systems.

In the coming years we will probably see a movement towards the use of Linux as an operating system. This is considered to be a stable system that offers good utilization of computer resources. It is also an open code system, which will allow each manufacturer to make changes to fit the needs of specific product or system.

New ways of distinguishing the background from the foreground will be used. Today the good-old chroma-key process is used. New methods are already introduced to improve performance of chroma-key systems. The TrueMatte system developed by the BBC's R&D department is an attempt to reduce the amount of lighting needed and put a small amount of blue light to work in a very efficient and precise way.

An interesting approach has been introduced by 3DV Systems. This is an add-on to any standard TV camera called ZCAM. The ZCAM uses infrared technology to measure in real time, for each pixel in the frame the distance of the object from the camera. In addition to the digital RGB information, it pro-

3-D video camera. Courtesy of 3DV Systems.

3-D video camera. Courtesy of 3DV Systems.

duces also depth (Z) information in 8 or 10 bits per pixel. Depth information is also available in the form of a B/W video stream where the luminance is relative to the depth or distance from the camera of each pixel in the frame. Depth information can be used to map the position of objects in the studio in real time. Such a system can not only distinguish between foreground and background, it can measure and map the position of each object in the studio. It can also differentiate between parts of the same object, if their distance from the camera is different. This can be used to place virtual objects in different places in 3-D space, directly related to the momentary position of performers in the studio.

Different effects where a virtual object will hide an actor and vice-versa were already demonstrated, performed in a dynamic, live way in a chroma-key-less environment. It is possible that such systems will be able to replace traditional chroma-key in TV studios.

Using motion-capture capabilities and virtual performers, we will probably see a growing number of productions where a combination of virtual set and virtual actors will be used. I believe that we will in a few years witness newscasts delivered by virtual news announcers and weather people, from a virtual, studio-less environment.

The virtual studio industry is at a turning point. By the end of 1999 the number of systems that have been sold is less than 200. Until now investing in a virtual studio system was considered by most decision makers to be an adventure. Manufacturers feel that even though the technology has been here for a few years, only in the second half of 1999 did it become accepted as a valuable and productive technology. Manufacturers tend to believe that from the year 2000 onwards, sales graphs will show increased sales figures.

The possibility to use small studios and limited funds to build sets that make the program look big and fancy, will prevail. Producers will not be able to ignore this potential.

In terms of pricing, it is safe to say that the price of all levels of virtual studio systems will come down. Some companies such as Intergraph and Sun intend to produce new high-end graphic platforms, which will cause competition and reduce prices of the most expensive part of virtual studio systems.

This may seem a bit farfetched, but I will not be surprised if virtual studio systems for use with home computers and simple video cameras will be introduced in a few years. This will allow production of home videos where the background of the picture is taken from still pictures, graphics or another home video.

Overview of Available
Virtual Studio Products

The worldwide market of virtual studio systems is not very large. Only a handful of manufacturers offer complete systems. Some manufacturers offer one or two sets while others have a wider selection of systems to offer.

In the following appendix, presented in alphabetical order, you will find descriptions of various virtual studio products, as published by the manufacturers in various publications. Any opinions expressed in this section are those of the manufacturers unless otherwise indicated.

Accom

Accom, headquartered in Menlo Park, California, designs, manufactures, sells, and supports a complete line of digital video production, recording and editing tools, and the ELSET virtual set systems, for the worldwide professional television production, postproduction, broadcasting, and computer video marketplaces.

Accom is a world leader in digital video technology for television broadcasting, computer video, production, and postproduction. We are the manufacturer of products designed for use today and into the next century.

Revolutionary

Accom's products have changed the way professional video is produced, and are in use all over the world.

Award-Winning

Our products have received numerous awards and citations from industry associations, publications, and customers, including two Emmys and three International Teleproduction Society Monitor awards for Engineering Excellence.

Respected

Accom's founders and its employees are comprised of the most tenured and respected people in the television industry, many of them instrumental in developing products that have set benchmarks for excellence.

Customer-Oriented

Accom is renowned for excellence in sales support and service, with a large technical support staff and over 150 distributors in every corner of the globe.

Accom, headquartered in Menlo Park, California, was established in 1988, and has demonstrated considerable growth since that time. Accom is committed not only to excellence in manufacturing, but also to a creative work environment, competitive compensation, and a wide array of benefits. The company became public in 1995 (OTC trading symbol: ACMM), and is the manufacturer of a full line of products that target various areas of the professional video marketplace.

ACCOM ELSET PRODUCTS

ELSET<u>LIVE</u> License—*"Synchronous Cuts"* for up to 4 cameras. An unlimited number of cameras may be supported. Dynamic synchronous switching allows any of the cameras to display the virtual set, but only one camera at a time can view the virtual set (no preview).

"Preview/Dissolve"—system for dissolving between two live cameras both within the virtual set environment. This configuration requires two graphics "pipelines" using a rack Onyx or two Deskside Onyx systems. A redundancy option is also available when using a Preview/Dissolve system with two Deskside Onyx systems.

❖ Import of 3-D models in either DXF or Inventor format. ELSET<u>LIVE</u> can read 3-D models from: Alias/Wavefront, Maya, Autocad, 3D Studio/MAX, Softimage.

❖ Import of textures created using a scanner or paint package such as Matador or Photoshop.

❖ Extensive library of 20 sample sets that may be used directly or easily modified and transformed into new sets.

❖ AutoTEX—Combines the Map Set with automated texture rendering scripts. MapSet provides tools for either manual or automated object regrouping, manual or automated texture mapping, and automatic generation of texture rendering scripts. Texture rendering scripts for various rendering packages such as Lightscape, Alias, Maya, Softimage, TDI Explore, TBT, and Wavefront Explore are supported. The concept behind AutoTEX is to merge the sophisticated lighting environments available in the packages described above with the base textures defined in the virtual set. This provides wonderful and realistic lighting in a virtual set while still running in real time.

The sophisticated scripting interface of ELSET<u>LIVE</u>, called ScriptSet, allows the user to trigger real time events occurring on the set. These events include:

• movements of objects on the set (translation, rotation, scaling, etc.)
• change of attributes (transparency, distance key, etc.)
• hide and show objects
• physically based multiplane defocusing
• video textures on/off
• sound effects
• swapping of multilayered (3-D) textures
• unlimited event functions linked to user defined production panel
• saving and restoring of event states
• object grouping
• import of camera flight paths from Alias
• import of complex hierarchical object animations from Alias
• environment mapping—reflections
• inclusion of other script files

❖ The Infinite blue-box feature allows the camera operators to go beyond the physical limits of the blue box while still displaying the virtual set. This feature is particularly useful in displaying virtual ceilings or true 360 degree views of your virtual set. Note that no real objects or actors can be keyed in the part of the image that stands outside of the blue box boundaries.

❖ CameraSet interfaces with the cameras and reads in real time the camera and lens parameters: X,Y,Z, pan, tilt, zoom, focus. Through an accurate calibration procedure it takes into account the nonlinearity of the lenses. This eliminates artifacts when the camera or lens moves (perfect synchronization of the virtual and real world). It allows for creation of sets that mix complex real props with the virtual set without the real props shifting or floating. It also allows for the shadows of the real props or actors to be properly projected on the virtual set. Up to 20 real cameras can be connected to the ELSET^{LIVE} system. A PC is required for each set of four real cameras.

❖ The real time rendering module of the ELSET^{LIVE} system displays the set in real time according to the camera movements. It also modifies the set according to the event triggered by the operator (ScriptSet play mode). This module outputs a video signal that is sent to the keyer and switcher.

❖ The ELSET^{LIVE} production control panel GUI simplifies the program production. All program events may be set up as sequential or individually activated events and triggered from GUI. The advantage of sequentially defined events is simplicity. The Elset operator needs to only press one and the same button to activate each event during the show. Individually activated events may be triggered any time and in any order. This feature is useful during show rehearsals or none scripted shows.

❖ Support for dual video input (requires second DIVO board).

❖ Real time virtual shadow which projects the talent's shadow onto any virtual object with no delay. The edges of the calibrated shadow may be softened and the shadow intensity modified.

Customer site survey to insure proper integration:

❖ Produce a list of all available equipment.

❖ Determine which if any additional equipment is needed prior to the ELSET system installation.

The software installation on the Onyx and PC

Complete system calibration including:

❖ Lens calibration for up to four lenses.

❖ Camera calibration.

One PC with special serial connection to interface up to four data head outputs to the Onyx(es)

Recommendations/consulting on third party equipment for the virtual set:

❖ Chroma key set

❖ Lighting

❖ Chroma-keyers

❖ Switchers

❖ Delays

❖ Audio

❖ Cameras

❖ Camera heads (all commercially available tracking systems are supported) lenses (Fujinon or Canon ENG lens—sensors must be mounted for zoom and focus)

❖ Video sources and synchronization

On-site final integration and tuning

On site training for two persons:

❖ Virtual set graphics designer with knowledge of 3-D modelers and SGI Graphics/UNIX.

❖ ELSET computer operator with knowledge in video.

ELSET Options

"Distance-Key" allows the actors to disappear or partially disappear behind virtual objects.

"Sound effects" allow sounds to be triggered by an event in the ELSET Script. These sound effects are thus always perfectly synchronized with any other event occurring on the virtual set.

"Defocus" allows the creation and animation of sets that are not always focused. The amount of defocus varies in real time as a function of the zoom and the focus of a given camera.

"Camera Preview" provides a camera preview (not air quality) running on an SGI O2 or SGI Impact workstation. Each preview allows an off-air camera to display the correct camera angle of the virtual set as a preview. In addition, when using the Impact video in an Impact workstation, internal chroma-keying is provided. This option requires an additional SGI O2 and copy of ELSET Preview software for each additional camera preview desired.

"Preview/Dissolve System" allows for two simultaneous streams (requires two desksides or a rack Onyx) that may be dissolved between in a live production. Redundancy option is available which allows "Synchronous Cuts" operation in the event of a failure.

Third Party Equipment:

The following equipment is required in addition to the ELSET software:

❖ SGI Onyx2 IR

❖ Chroma-key studio

❖ Lighting grid

❖ Lighting

❖ Cameras with lenses

❖ Camera heads as specified

❖ Tripods or pedestals

❖ Video delays (typically 2 frames per camera)

❖ Video playback for live video textures

❖ Audio delays (if needed)

❖ Audio playback system

❖ Chroma-keyers

❖ Switcher

❖ Cabling

❖ 3-D modeler software such as Alias/Wavefront, Maya, Autocad, Softimage, 3-D Max, etc. Software packages such as these are necessary for modeling the geometry of the virtual sets

❖ Paint package such as Matador, Photoshop, Illustrator. Software packages such as these are necessary for texture creation and retouching

❖ Workstations or PCs to run 3-D modeler and paint package

❖ SGI Onyx2 Infinite Reality (Synchronous Cuts System): 2 R10000 CPUs, 2 RM7's each with 64 MB Texture Memory, DIVO Video with serial I/O, GVO Video with serial output, 512 MB system memory, DAT, CD-ROM, 4 Gig System Disk. Deskside or Rack configurations may be used.

A typical Preview/Dissolve ELSET system requires two Deskside Onyx systems configured as above.

Preview Hardware Configuration

SGI O2 for ELSET's Camera Preview Option: 175 MHz R5000 CPU, 128 MB system memory, 2 to 4 Gig System Disk.

General Requirements

Because virtual sets require a new area of expertise which is not always found in the television/broadcasting environment, Virtual Set customers should commit employees with the appropriate background to be trained on the Accom system during the initial training and during any other relevant training. Two profiles can be defined which require two sets of complementary expertise:

Virtual Set Designer
❖ General proficiency in UNIX
❖ SGI 3-D graphics, Performer and Inventor
❖ Experience in 3-D modeling
❖ Experience in paint packages

Virtual Set Engineer
❖ Expertise in video equipment: switchers, keyers, delays
❖ Knowledge of UNIX
❖ Knowledge of motorized camera heads
❖ Proficient in communication software between computer equipment

Elset Unique Features

Software:

❖ Ability to import many file formats—The philosophy adopted during the design of Elset was to provide a completely open virtual set system which could communicate with as many modeling, animation, and lighting packages on the market as possible. The objective was to allow users to design their virtual environments with the tools they are already familiar with and tap into the strengths of each one of these packages. ELSET<u>LIVE</u> can read 3-D models from: Alias/Wavefront, Maya, Autocad, 3-D Studio/MAX, Softimage, Multigen, and Lightscape.

❖ Automated Texture Rendering (AutoTex)—Providing an excellent lighting environment in the virtual set is one of the most important aspects in creating a realistic looking virtual set. The concept behind AutoTEX is to automatically merge the sophisticated lighting environments which may be created in various rendering packages, with the unlit base textures assigned in the virtual set modeler. AutoTEX automatically creates texture rendering scripts for various rendering packages such as Lightscape, Alias (PowerAnimator & Maya), Softimage, TDI Explore, TBT, and Wavefront Explore. This process allows you to preserve the wonderful and realistic lighting of the rendered set for the real time virtual set without requiring any texture painting. AutoTEX rendering scripts are created using the MapSet tools. These MapSet tools provide for either manual or automated object regrouping, sophisticated manual texture mapping, automated texture mapping, and automatic generation of texture rendering scripts.

Extensive scripting GUI

The sophisticated scripting interface of ELSET<u>LIVE</u>, called ScriptSet, allows the user to trigger real time events occurring on the set. These events include:

1) Movements of objects on the set (translation, rotation, scaling, etc.)
2) Change of attributes (transparency blending, etc.)
3) "Distance-Key" (D-Key) allows the actors to disappear or partially disappear behind virtual objects
4) Hide and show virtual objects with time controllable dissolve option
5) Physically based multiplane defocusing based on zoom and focus camera data
6) Video textures on/off on any number of objects of any shape or size
7) Sound effects
8) Swapping of multilayered (3-D) textures with time controlled blending or cuts between layers
9) Unlimited event functions linked to user defined production panel
10) Saving and restoring of event states
11) Object grouping
12) Automatic import of camera flight paths from Alias and SoftImage
13) Automatic import of complex hierarchical object animations from Alias (PowerAnimator & Maya) and SoftImage
14) Inclusion of other script files
15) System performance optimization tools

Interactive and easy to use production panel

The ELSET<u>LIVE</u> production control panel GUI simplifies the program production. All program events may be set up as sequential or individually activated events and triggered from GUI. The advantage of sequentially defined events is simplicity. The Elset operator needs to only press one and the same button to activate each event during the show. Individually activated events may be triggered any time and in any order. This feature is useful during show rehearsals or none scripted shows.

Import of complex hierarchical animations

The internally defined Elset scripting tools satisfy nearly all animation requirements in a virtual set. Now and then users wish to perform complex hierarchical animations in real time as well. Elset gives you this option. Due to the extensive communication between Elset and Alias or SoftImage you may use the power of these two animation packages to define sophisticated animations and export them to Elset. An easy to use Elset GUI automatically extracts all defined animation paths from the animation package, precomputes the transformation matrix for each hierarchical node for all keyframes, and saves this information to an animation file. During production these animation files are executed in real time enabling you to run complex hierarchical animations with no computational overhead in the Elset environment.

BlueBox GUI

The BlueBox GUI provides many options to create a model of your studio blue box, which will be used as an infinite blue-box. Options for one-, two-, or three-wall studios, specification of wall and cove dimensions, as well as shadow safe zones are provided. The infinite blue-box feature allows the camera operators to go beyond the physical limits of the blue box while still displaying the virtual set. This feature is particularly useful in displaying virtual ceilings or true 360 degree views of your virtual set.

Interactive positioning and orientation of the virtual set

Elset's PositionSet module is interactive GUI allowing the user to quickly position and orientate the virtual set with respect to the studio blue box. The GUI consists of a plan view showing you the location of all defined real cameras, the studio blue box and the moveable floor plan of the virtual set. To properly establish the position of the virtual set a perspective view from the active camera's point of view with keyed foreground is displayed.

Interactive camera definition and camera matching tool

Elset's CameraSet module is an interactive GUI allowing the user to define and accurately position virtual cameras matching up to 20 studio cameras with respect to a studio reference point. The user may interactively switch between all defined cameras to verify correct inter-camera positioning and display all available views to the producer. Combined with the PositionSet module these tools deliver a cohesive reference of the real and virtual worlds for an unlimited number of set positions and camera configurations. All calibrated references may be saved to files to be recalled latter.

Defocus based on true camera data

The 1996 NAB award winning defocus tool available in the Elset software is to date still the only depth of field software based on true camera data. The amount of defocus varies in real time as a function of the zoom and the focus data of a given camera. The amount of background defocus can truly match the physical defocus of the foreground. Rack focus between foreground and background is fully supported.

Virtual Shadow

This option projects the talent's shadow in real-time onto any virtual object with no delay. The edges of the calibrated shadow may be softened and the shadow intensity modified.

Environment Mapping

This feature adds to the realism created by the ELSET<u>LIVE</u> system, the simulation of reflections from the surrounding environment onto objects is provided.

Character Animation

ELSET<u>LIVE</u> provides integration with popular character animation software. This allows virtual sets to be combined with live character animation while both track camera movements.

Application Programmers Interface (API)

Elset's elaborate API allows customers or third party developers to link their software with Elset. Elset also accepts shared databases allowing the virtual set and an external database such as business graphics, weather graphics, election data, or character animation to simultaneously track the camera movements. Full integration of the D-Key is supported for objects in an external database.

System Feedback

Elset's ConfigSet GUI allows the user to configure the setup of the entire system. Elset also provides a Message Viewer GUI that receives feedback from all modules of the system and allows the user to filter them according to time, source, etc. This valuable information may be displayed as messages to the user upon request.

Hardware:

Synchronous Cuts for multiple cameras

Elset provides "Synchronous Cuts" for up to four cameras. Synchronous cuts may be extended to up to 12 cameras by simply adding an additional PCs.

Preview Dissolve System

The "Preview/Dissolve" option enables dissolving between two live cameras both within the virtual set environment. This configuration requires two graphics "pipelines" using a rack Onyx or two Deskside Onyx systems. A redundancy option is also available when using a Preview / Dissolve system with two Deskside Onyx systems.

Accom lens calibration and camera tracking software

Over the years Accom has evolved Elset's lens calibration and camera tracking software to provide the best camera tracking in the industry. The "CameraSet" tool interfaces with the cameras and reads in real time the camera and lens parameters: X,Y,Z, pan, tilt, zoom, focus. Through an accurate calibration procedure it takes into account the nonlinearity of the lenses. This eliminates artifacts when the camera or lens moves (perfect synchronization of the virtual and real world). It allows for creation of sets that mix complex real props with the virtual set without the real props shifting or floating. It also allows for the shadows of the real props or actors to be properly projected on the virtual set. Up to 20 real cameras can be connected to the ELSET^{LIVE} system. Camera sensor information from four cameras is processed by one inexpensive PC. The advantage of using a PC is all the CPU power of the graphics engine is dedicated to the virtual set.

Interactive camera switcher GUI

Elset's camera switcher GUI gives the operator the ability to switch defined cameras for a one or multiple graphics pipe system at any instant. Switching, however, is not restricted to this GUI. Elset's communication with switchers supporting the GVG 100/200, GVG TenXL, Sierra Video Systems, and Leitch protocols enables switching from the control room as well. Elset's production panel also allows the user to assign events to camera cuts. When a camera is switched, a user-defined event is automatically triggered.

Integration to a range of camera tracking systems

Elset's open architecture philosophy was also extended to communicating with various tracking systems. Elset has interfaced to all of the tracking systems listed below.

❖ BBC Free *d pattern recognition system
❖ Thoma Walkfinder
❖ Vinten Vector 70 (Thoma sensors)
❖ Radamec (mobile & pedestal)
❖ Ultimatte Memory Head
❖ Panther Crane & Dolly
❖ DMC/Xync
❖ Evans & Sutherland
❖ ATM
❖ Hybrid MC

Ability to communicate to many external devices

The same open architecture philosophy was applied to communicating with numerous external devices such as:

❖ Integration of Accom's Axess & WSD/Xtreme. ELSET<u>LIVE</u> is the only virtual set to offer integration of stills and real-time video/key/audio clips. Perfect for all prerecorded roll-ins.

❖ Ultimatte Keyer Control. ELSET<u>LIVE</u> provides serial control of the Ultimatte 8 to enable gradual or immediate transitions from one setting to another. This gives the ability to mimic virtual lighting changes in the physical or "real" world.

❖ Router and Switcher Control. ELSET<u>LIVE</u> provides serial control of various routers and switchers to trigger the crosspoints. This gives the power of switching control from various external devices.

❖ Control of camera tally lights. When switching between the various cameras ELSET<u>LIVE</u> automatically triggers the appropriate tally lights.

❖ Communication with driver devices such as the Spaceball. The communication with the Spaceball enables users to easily fly through the virtual set or position objects in the virtual set to any location.

❖ Ability to provide low cost camera preview. The "Camera Preview" provides a camera preview (not air quality) running on an SGI O2 workstation. Each preview allows an off-air camera to display the correct camera angle of the virtual set as a preview keyed with the foreground.

ELSET<u>LIVE-NT</u>—LIVE Virtual Set on NT Platform

General information:

ELSET <u>LIVE-NT</u> is a 3-D virtual set solution with robust features such as live video I/O, Distance Key, Infinite Blue Box, and, of course, ELSET picture quality. It runs on today's low-cost, high-performance visual workstations and a WindowsNT operating system. ELSET <u>LIVE-NT</u> was designed with many plug-in components that allow 3-D Studio MAX to function as the "front end" to the ELSET environment.

Sets, scenes and environments for ELSET <u>LIVE-NT</u> are created and animated using 3-D Studio MAX. With over 90,000 copies of 3-D Studio MAX sold, chances are you already know someone who can build your first ELSET virtual set.

Specific features:

❖ Authoring your sets on 3-D Studio MAX®, ELSET <u>LIVE-NT</u> uses 3-D Studio MAX as the "front end" to the ELSET environment. All tools and plug-ins available in 3-D Studio MAX are for use in the virtual set. Animations can easily be defined and executed in real time.

❖ ELSET <u>LIVE-NT</u> uses the same Accom-exclusive texture processing tools as ELSET <u>LIVE</u>. ELSET's AutoTex tool allows you to preserve the exact qualities and attributes of the renderer in the authoring software, instead of having to use inaccurate and cartoon-like hardware rendered scenes from the host computer. AutoTex automatically renders texture maps to objects in a virtual scene, enhancing the look of the finished set. AutoTex gives Accom's ELSET the highest quality of any virtual set today. Plus you can use all 3-D Studio MAX plug-ins and renderers, providing unparalleled flexibility in your virtual set productions.

❖ Real-time 3-D System E ELSET <u>LIVE-NT</u> operates at a true 50/60 Hz. Anti-aliased scenes—Scenes rendered with ELSET <u>LIVE-NT</u> are antialiased eliminating the undesirable "jaggies" typical of computer generated non-anti-aliased images.

❖ Live Video Input/Output—With ELSET <u>LIVE-NT</u> live video panels or textures can be incorporated into scenes, complete with camera position information. The studio operator has complete control over the camera as well as the virtual set during the actual production.

❖ ELSET <u>LIVE-NT</u> uses Accoms' accurate lens calibration files—Accom offers an unmatched level of accuracy for camera lens calibration to ELSET virtual sets. Access to an extensive library of calibrated camera lens files as part of the ELSET installation. The real set position of floors, walls and objects are also calibrated to the virtual set so that any camera or live movement is seamless and realistic.

❖ Tracking systems—As with all ELSET products, ELSET <u>LIVE-NT</u> allows you to interface with practically all tracking systems available on the market.

❖ Distance Key—Talent can move behind and be partially or fully obscured by objects in the virtual set. This places talent in a true 3-D environment, as opposed to merely compositing them against a virtual background.

❖ Infinite Blue Box—Virtual sets can be as large as you like without regard to the physical limits of your studio. This allows you to view ceilings and with 360 degree pans, show pieces of the virtual set that exist behind the camera.

❖ Open Architecture—The ELSET <u>LIVE-NT</u> system was developed using standard platform concepts. Because of its open architecture, the ELSET <u>LIVE-NT</u> system will grow as future task-specific modules are developed. ELSET <u>LIVE-NT</u> will allow you to continue to take advantage of enhancements in 3-D modeling, computer processing speed, and platform costs.

❖ Interface to Accom DDRs – With ELSET <u>LIVE-NT</u> you can randomly access and control playout of prerecorded video clips as part of your virtual set production.

ELSET <u>LIVE-NT</u> License

❖ Single camera system. Generates the virtual set background for your camera views in real time 60/50 Hz.

❖ Import of 3-D models from 3-D Studio MAX.

❖ Live video in. Allows you to play two live video sources inside of the virtual set. The video may be mapped onto any set geometry.

❖ The Infinite blue-box feature allows the camera operators to go beyond the physical limits of the blue box while still displaying the virtual set. This feature is particularly useful in displaying virtual ceilings. Note that no real objects or actors can be keyed in the part of the image that stands outside of the blue box boundaries. In this mode, the second video channel may not be displayed.

❖ CameraSet interfaces with the cameras and reads in real time the camera and lens parameters: X,Y,Z, pan, tilt, zoom, focus. Through an accurate calibration procedure it takes into account the nonlinearity of the lenses. This eliminates artifacts when the camera or lens moves (perfect synchronization of the virtual and real world). It allows for creation of sets that mix complex real props with the virtual set without the real props shifting or floating.

❖ The ELSET<u>LIVE-NT</u> displays the set in real time according to the camera movements.

Complete system calibration including:

❖ Lens calibration for one lens.

❖ Camera calibration.

ELSET<u>LIVE-NT</u> Options

❖ Multicamera Synchronous Cuts system provides dynamic synchronous switching capability for multiple cameras to display the virtual set. Only one camera at a time can view the virtual set.

❖ Preview/Dissolve System provides a second live graphics video channel for Preview / Dissolve operation allowing you to dissolve between two cameras in a live production. This system can also be used as a preview system giving the camera operator a composite preview for framing the next shot.

❖ Distance Keying and Infinite Blue Box. Distance Keying allows the talent to be behind virtual objects in the set. The Infinite Blue-Box feature allows the camera operators to go beyond the physical limits of the blue box while still displaying the virtual set. This feature is particularly useful in displaying virtual ceilings. Note that no real objects or actors can be keyed in the part of the image that stands outside of the blue box boundaries. This option requires a chroma-keyer with external matte input.

Required Third Party Software
The following software is required in addition to the E ELSET LIVE-NT software:

❖ 3-D Studio Max authoring software

Required Third Party Equipment
The following equipment is required in addition to the ELSET LIVE-NT software:

❖ SGI 540 Visual Workstation
❖ Camera Tracking (recommend: Radamec VR Pan and Tilt Head with zoom and focus sensors)
❖ Lighting grid
❖ Lighting
❖ Camera(s) with Fuji or Canon ENG lenses
❖ Tripods or pedestals
❖ Video delay (two frames) per camera depending on camera tracking system
❖ Chroma-keyer with external key (matte) input
❖ Converters (AD)
❖ For multiple camera systems, a switcher or router for switching between cameras

General Requirements:
Because virtual sets require a new area of expertise that is not always found in the typical environments, the customer should plan on employees with the appropriate background to be trained on the Accom system during the initial training and during any other relevant training.

Two profiles can be defined requiring two sets of complementary expertise:

Virtual Set Designer
❖ Expertise in 3-D modeling
❖ Experience in paint packages
❖ Expertise in 3-D StudioMax

Virtual Set Engineer
❖ Expertise in video equipment: switchers, keyers, delays
❖ Knowledge of NT systems
❖ Knowledge on motorized camera heads
❖ Proficient in communication software between computer equipment

ELSET<u>POST</u> – Virtual Set for low-cost SGI Computers

General information:
ELSET<u>POST</u> enables video producers to shoot their productions while seeing a preview of the live scenes using a low cost Silicon Graphics (SGI) computer system. ELSET<u>POST</u> uses Alias or Maya as the front end to create the set and view scenes during production. During production, accurately calibrated camera moves, in addition to live animation triggers, are recorded with time code on the SGI. After production the scene is automatically rebuilt with the recorded camera path and time accurate animations. The virtual scenes are rendered on any Silicon Graphics workstation or server, and then recorded to Accom's WSD/2Xtreme. Through integration with the WSD/2Xtreme, postproduction is easily automated. By rendering the virtual scenes offline, even the most complex scenes with ray tracing and particle animation can be produced which are not possible in real-time virtual set productions.

Specific features:
❖ Highest quality—lowest cost! The ELSET<u>POST</u> system uses Maya or Alias PowerAnimator as the front end. These two packages are recognized worldwide as producing the highest quality scenes. ELSET<u>POST</u> may run on low-cost workstations like the SGI O2 or Octane during production and rendering of these beautifully defined scenes.
❖ Tracking systems—As with all Elset products ELSET<u>POST</u> allows you to interface to practically all tracking system available on the market.
❖ Calibrated camera tracking with time code—During production, accurately calibrated camera moves are recorded with time code in real time. This process incorporates the calibrated lens information originally developed

and refined in the high end ELSET<u>LIVE</u> system. The recorded camera tracking data assures that the perspective views of the virtual backgrounds are identical to the perspective views of the recorded foreground.

❖ Preview of the virtual background ELSET<u>POST</u> provides a live interactive preview of the virtual background while recording the foreground information. The virtual background keyed with the talent foreground enables the director to correctly frame his or her shots. In addition, the talent sees the location of the virtual objects with which interaction is desired.

❖ Automatic postproduction rendering—Once the shooting of the foreground is completed no additional work on the scene is required. The scene is automatically rebuilt with the recorded camera path and time accurate animations. The time code assures perfect synchronization of foreground and background frames.

❖ Distance key—Maintains the proper priority of objects and actors within the set, allowing "real" elements to appear in front or behind virtual elements based upon their true position in the scene.

❖ Advanced animations—ELSET<u>POST</u> can trigger all object animations, including inverse kinematics, from within the 3-D package when the director wants them to occur. These triggers are saved with the same time code as the camera data. During the rendering phase the animations are rendered at the exact same time when the director called them. You also have the possibility to use every sophisticated rendering features of Alias/Maya such as bumps and ray tracing, as well as particle animations to produce effects such as fire and water. These advanced features are not available in real-time virtual sets software.

❖ Infinite Blue Box—Virtual sets can be as large as you like without regard to the physical limits of your studio. ELSET's Infinite Blue Box allows the camera to still "see" the virtual environment when panning and tilting past the physical limits of the blue or green stage—a full 360 degrees!

❖ Flexibility—ELSET<u>POST</u> you may shoot your foreground using an unfinished set and renders the scene once the set is completed. In addition, it is possible to repeat rendering with modified or different sets from those used for shooting, without the necessity to rehire your actors and reshoot the foreground.

ELSET POST License

❖ ELSET<u>POST</u> Alias or Maya plug-in. Some sets are too complicated to run in real time even on the most powerful Onyx platforms. By using ELSET<u>POST</u>

even the most complicated of sets can be used for virtual set productions. Once the production has been shot, scenes too complicated to be rendered by ELSET<u>LIVE</u> can be postproduced using the ELSET<u>POST</u> process. This approach gives the program producer the greatest degree of freedom possible in creating productions.

❖ CameraSet interfaces with the cameras and reads in real time the camera and lens parameters: X,Y,Z, pan, tilt, zoom, focus. Through an accurate calibration procedure it takes into account the nonlinearity of the lenses. This eliminates artifacts when the camera or lens moves (perfect synchronization of the virtual and real world). It allows for creation of sets that mix complex real props with the virtual set without the real props shifting or floating.

Complete system calibration including:
❖ Lens calibration, 1 lens.
❖ Camera calibration.

Required Third Party Equipment:
The following equipment is required in addition to the ELSET software:
❖ Silicon Graphics O2 as follows:
  • 175 MHz R5000 CPU, 128 MB system memory, 2 to 4 Gig System Disk
  • Alias Animation software for set design
❖ Camera tracking System for pan, tilt, zoom, focus, x, y, z, and roll
❖ Accom 2Xtreme Digital Disk Recorder for recording rendered background
❖ Lighting grid
❖ Lighting
❖ Camera(s) with Fuji or Canon ENG lenses
❖ Tripods or pedestals
❖ Chroma-keyer for previewing (camera over nonreal-time background from O2)

Evans & Sutherland

Creativity without Limits

There's no limit to the content you can create using a virtual studio system. The E&S MindSet System allows live talent to seamlessly interact with environments and elements generated in many of today's popular 3-D modeling programs. Virtual and real sets can be combined to achieve the look you need. Individual elements can easily be moved and changed.

Whether your field is broadcast television or video production, you'll find that it's easy to create the high-quality visual content you and your clients demand—in hours rather than days or weeks.

Imagine the possibilities—set objects in motion, integrate live video anywhere in your scene, and create dynamic special effects. Whatever you want, you can make it happen with the affordable, reliable, flexible power of the E&S MindSet System.

❖ Running a local TV station? Boost your ratings by adding new life to news and sports with exciting sets and backdrops. Make your weather forecast the one everyone watches—and understands.

❖ Creating educational or corporate videos? Focus your viewer's attention and explain complex concepts more easily by walking them through a virtual object. Go anywhere, see anything—broadcast live from Mars or explore inside a human heart. The possibilities are endless.

The exceptional quality and realism of 3-D environments rendered in real time by the power of the E&S MindSet Virtual Studio System will make an incredible impact on your audience. The high quality interactive lighting, surface textures, and animation are an integral part of the realism of the scene and open up whole new virtual worlds to your viewers.

Reliability at an Affordable Price

The E&S MindSet Virtual Studio System introduces a totally new dimension in performance at an unheard-of price point—extremely affordable and competitive. Its plug-ins for popular NT-based graphics programs and compatibility with your studio equipment make very efficient use of the resources you already have.

You'll find that the system will quickly pay for itself by allowing faster program development and reducing expensive studio time. Sets can be designed, built, animated, and dressed completely on a computer screen, then struck in a few keystrokes, stored on disk, and easily sent to other studios. Location costs diminish as set designers, freed from limits of sound stages, can easily recreate large environments such as full-sized football stadiums in a small studio.

The E&S MindSet System is designed for the high-pressure working environment of today's TV and video production operations. It is easy to use, practical, and fast. For instance, four-point camera calibration allows you to quickly relocate your camera and calibrate within seconds, and the FuseBox "Virtual Technician" online troubleshooting feature lets you know when something requires attention, how severe the condition is, and how to resolve it.

As Evans & Sutherland's clients in the aerospace and space technology industries can attest, we are in a unique position to understand the necessity of reliability and the importance of high-quality maintenance. Many of our products are literally "mission critical" so exceptional technical support is part of our corporate way of life. We have a reputation for technical excellence and innovation that spans three decades, and we are constantly working to push the boundaries of technology and enhance the capabilities of our products.

E&S Mindset Virtual Studio System features:

❖ Windows NT based—Familiar interface with open architecture

❖ Unique anti-aliased video texture allows live video in scene

❖ Fusebox Control Software that has offline rehearsal capability

❖ Virtual Sets can be designed in popular modeling packages

❖ Virtual Cameras that can be linked with real cameras

❖ Guaranteed frame rates from Graphics Supercomputer

❖ MindSet LC provides low cost preview functionality

❖ Real-time sub-pixel anti-aliasing to eliminate moving lines

❖ True 3-D that allows talent to "walk around" objects

❖ Environment mapping for reflections

❖ Up to four texture maps per polygon

❖ Offline rehearsal capability

❖ Virtual cameras linked with real cameras

❖ Camera Calibration in less than a minute

❖ Extremely precise camera tracking

❖ Garbage matte channel allows 360 degree shots

❖ Variable video delay with built-in converter

❖ 19" rack mountable

❖ Fully integrated system

GETRIS

PSYset the trackless virtual set
PSYset approaches the virtual set challenge from an entirely new direction. Using real-stationary cameras, PSYset virtually simulates studio camera moves, without any camera-tracking systems, giving your virtual sets depth and realism. Compact and very easy to set-up, PSYset is designed for both on-site and off-site broadcast. Cost-effective and easy-to-use, PSYset can change your studio look in minutes and fascinate your viewers for hours.

Simulate camera motion and immerse talents in 3-D scenery
With its patented trackless technology, PSYset uses the output of fixed studio cameras to generate multiple camera perspectives, including zooms in and out, pans and tilts. Ideal for small sets, PSYset's applications include talk shows, news, sports and weather reports and provide unmatched performance at a breakthrough price.

Easy to set-up and easy to use, PSYset makes virtual set a reality
With no expensive tracking devices to calibrate and no video delays, PSYset is up and running with just a few minutes of set-up time. With its portable hardware low maintenance requirements, and use of standard cameras, PSYset is a practical and productive tool for broadcasters.

Insert live video streams to give life to synthetic sets
PSYset delivers an exceptional level of real-time rendering and video compositing: up to four D1 images can be instantly combined with real-time 3-D graphics, thanks to the PSY engine unique architecture for uncompressed video mapping (video+key).

Optimize your investment with an integrated system
With its integrated 3-D DVE, CG and stillstore, PSYset provides an extensive toolset for day-to-day use in the broadcast environment. Just like normal sets, virtual technology requires real-time transitions, shoulder boxes, text and so forth: PsySet gives all these under a single interface. What's more, during the time when the virtual set is not used, PSYset can be used for video effects in traditional sets.

PSYset features
❖ True 3-D polygon-based real-time virtual set animation
❖ Eight cameras supported in the standard version
❖ Built-in camera switch with effects

❖ One D1 video+key input for the anchorman, one D1 video+key input for a video screen in the set, one background video

❖ Up to four quarters of screen resolution D1 inputs (hypervideo option)

❖ Two frames audio delay (no video delay)

❖ Character generation with Inscriber software

❖ Internal 15 minutes uncompressed storage (optional key and audio)

❖ On-air control & last minute modifications using VirtualFX "Set" software

❖ 14 to 16 screen-size graphics of texture memory

❖ Two directional lights, one ambient light with Phong method

❖ Field-based rendering with Phong shading

❖ Camera view, and effects playlist management

❖ GPI for synchronization to/of external system

❖ Audio jingle playback

❖ Dedicated keyboard for on-air operations

❖ All the features of PSYfx and PSYnews for simultaneous or sequential use on other TV programs

PSYset includes:

PSY 3-D virtual FX engine:

❖ Real-time MIPMAP builder with 10 bits internal processing per component

❖ One DIVI board for field interpolation, vertical and time-based filter

❖ One DVE A board: true 3-D geometrical engine, up to 840 megaflops CPU

❖ One DVE B board: lighting computation unit, Z buffer handling

❖ Two serial digital inputs, 10 bits, 4:2:2 & 4:0:0

❖ One serial digital input (background), 10 bits, 4:2:2

❖ One serial digital output, 10 bits, 4:2:2 & 4:0:0

❖ Dual 32 MB texture memory bank

❖ HPI board (PCI bus) for PSY workstation

❖ PSY video router (for up to eight cameras switch)

PSY workstation:

❖ Dual processor workstation with 128 MB ram, 4 GB HDD, CD-ROM, Ethernet, Keyboard, mouse; Windows NT 4.0. O/S

❖ Internal PSY DDR: 15 minutes of uncompressed video storage

PSYset software:

❖ Getris: Virtual FX "Set"

❖ Kinetix: 3-D Studio Max (with "Clothreyes" plug-in)

❖ Inscriber: title motion

PSYset Sensor-based virtual set

Virtual set technology is finally coming of age. By combining the open architecture of Windows NT with dedicated processing hardware, PSYset delivers a solution that is practical, powerful and affordable. PSYset unleashes the creativity of designers and producers, creating digital sets that can be modified in minutes.

❖ Design sets involving live video at a fraction of traditional costs.

❖ Video feeds are essential to creating ambiance in synthetic environments.

❖ Instead of reshaping standard workstations for video processing, the design of Psy specialized 10 bit video architecture enables the use of video walls, duplex in virtual sets, with a unique versatility and comfort.

❖ Combine proven camera tracking with PSYset realtime rendering.

❖ PSYset can be easily combined with off-the-shelf Radamec camera heads, using the PSYset calibration module. The initial setup and installation includes a straightforward, once-and-for-all calibration process. Afterwards, cameras can be operated in the usual way.

Make it virtual and keep it real

A virtual set system must integrate seamlessly with the equipment mix and workflow of today's broadcast operations. Production staffers and on-camera talent need to be comfortable with the tools they are using, not worrying for instance about important video delays. Keying must be fast and clean. PSYset was designed to meet these needs.

Use a versatile solution that matches all your needs

Why move to a virtual set system, unless it can both deliver what you can't achieve with a real set and give you the tools you are used to? PSYset enables you to create a virtual world filled with live video streams, real-time graphics and moving 3-D objects. PSYset is a real-time powerhouse for creating virtual sets, as well as news graphics, titles and live DVE moves.

PSYset s.b. key features

❖ True 3-D polygon-based real-time virtual set animation

❖ Two cameras supported in the standard version

❖ Two D1 video+key inputs for video screens in the set, one background video up to eight quarters of screen resolution D1 inputs (hypervideo option)

❖ Three frames audio and video delay

❖ Character generation with Inscriber software

❖ On-air control and last minute modifications using VirtualFX "Set" software

❖ 14 to 16 screen-size graphics of texture memory

❖ Two directional lights, one ambient light with Phong method

❖ Field-based rendering with Phong shading

❖ Camera view, and effects playlist management

❖ GPI for synchronization to/of external system

❖ Audio jingle playback

❖ Dedicated keyboard for on-air operations

❖ All the features of PSYfx and PSYnews for simultaneous or sequential use on other TV programs

PSYset s.b. includes:

❖ PSY 3-D virtual FX engine

❖ Real-time MIPMAP builder with 10 bits internal processing per component

❖ One DIVI board for field interpolation, vertical and time-based filter

❖ One DVE A board: true 3-D geometrical engine, up to 840 megaflops CPU

❖ One DVE B board: lighting computation unit, Z buffer handling

❖ Two serial digi-inputs, 10 bits, 4:2:2 & 4:0:0

❖ One serial digital input (background), 10 bits, 4:2:2

❖ One serial digital output, 10 bits, 42:2 & 4:0:0

❖ Dual 8 MB texture memory bank (upgradable to dual 32 MB)

❖ HPI board (PCI bus) for PSY workstation

PSYset video peripherals

❖ Two Radamec VR435 VRM with PSI and VR camera heads

❖ One tracking module

❖ One video delay

❖ One audio delay

❖ One digital chroma-keyer

❖ PSY integrated video router with remote control

❖ PSY workstation

❖ Dual processor workstation with 128 MB Ram, 4 GB HDD, CD-ROM, Ethernet Keyboard, mouse; Windows NT 4.0. O/S

PSYSET software

❖ Getris: Virtual FX "Set"

❖ Kinetix: 3-D Studio Max (with "Clothreyes" plug-in)

❖ Inscriber: title motion

ORAD

ORAD's mission is to realize the potential of proven and emerging electro-optical, video and real-time image processing technologies for TV broadcasting, Internet, production studio and sports events, enabling ORAD to provide a one stop technology shop for all it's customers

In these dynamic sectors and within a short period, ORAD has become the standard bearer through its virtual sets, sports commentary, virtual advertising and other innovative products.

Established in 1993, ORAD draws on the proven track records of experts in their field of specialization. ORAD's team operates at the vanguard of technology, harnessing powerful defense know-how to cutting edge commercial markets.

Real-time video processing and pattern recognition algorithms, powerful hardware engines, sophisticated sensor technologies and innovative application generators are being used to deliver unique tools that make TV, sports and advertising more exciting, effective, compelling and riveting.

ORAD's worldwide customer list includes the stars of the broadcasting and production markets. ORAD's award winning products receive frequent press coverage and are demonstrated at all major trade shows.

ORAD has partnered with ISL, the world's largest sports sponsorship group, representing international sports events worldwide. ISL holds the rights for several major international sports events, including the marketing rights for the 1998 Soccer World Cup and the broadcasting rights for the Soccer World Cups in 2002 and 2006. ISL has made a strong commitment to ORAD, taking equity in the company, and jointly marketing ORAD's virtual advertising systems.

ORAD is a member of the Ormat Group, a publicly traded conglomerate of companies engaged in optical inspection, alternative energy and sophisticated medical diagnostics.

ORAD's headquarters are in Kfar Saba, Israel with additional offices in the United States and Germany.

CyberSet's features:

CyberSet is not just the only virtual set based on pattern recognition. It is the most advanced system in the market as reflected by many other aspects:

❖ CyberSet is using a unique, automatic, "pixel-level" **Depth-Key module**, capable of continuously placing the actor in its right location in the virtual world. Depth-Key enables the creation of realistic perception of the image by allowing for the virtual objects and real objects and commentators occlude each other dynamically throughout the program. This is to be distinguished from the other systems using a manually operated "layer-level" depth key, wherein objects are classified into a restricted number of depth layers. The pixel-level depth key enables a much closer interaction between real and virtual objects; actors can not only walk behind or in front of objects, but may be inside them as well.

❖ Performance animated characters (**CyberActors**) can be integrated into the virtual studio using real-time motion capture. It is the first time that a performance animated character is integrated into a virtual set using a single rendering platform (Onyx) for both applications. It is also the first time that a motion captured actor is interacting with a real actor, using a common depth key—they can walk in front or behind each other and the proper depth key will be continuously applied. All this is done with a moving camera! CyberActor is a hard- ware/software add-on optional module to CyberSet.

❖ **Virtual Presence**—it is now possible to be in two places at one time with ORAD's Virtual Presence module. A live feed from a remote location is seamlessly incorporated into the "local" studio so that the remote actor becomes an integral part of the local set as a pseudo 3-D object. Virtual presence enables someone in a remote studio to interact with actors in the virtual set and not via video window. Guests on television shows will no longer have to travel to the "local" studio to be on the program. They will only have to travel to the nearest blue screen studio and then be added in real-time to the broadcast. Face-to-face discussions will be able to be conducted without the need for both parties to be in the same room together. The Virtual Presence module is offered as a free upgrade to CyberSet users.

❖ **Automatic Feedback/Marking system**—This innovative development from ORAD is designed to guide the presenter within the blue-screen environment with the momentary footprints and orientation of stationary and moving virtual objects projected onto the studio floor. The guidance system lets the presenter know where all the virtual objects are at all times. This feature is critical when virtual sets include animated objects or when sets are frequently changed. The Feedback/Marking system is an add-on optional module to CyberSet.

❖ **Depth of focus**—To give the sets a more realistic look, ORAD has addressed depth of focus of the "virtual" camera. Distant scene objects are blurred according to geometrical optics laws. The produced image is thus more realistic.

❖ **Shadow enhancement, foreground video manipulation & chroma-keying improvements**—ORAD's powerful multitasking, real-time video processor, the DVP 100, which is used to compute the camera's momentary viewpoint has been implemented with several complementary applications for virtual set and traditional productions. These applications greatly enhance CyberSet capabilities.

Firstly, the DVP 100 can be used to enhance the shadows cast on the studio floor by real objects giving a greater sense of photo-realism to the CyberSet production. This is done in real-time employing image-understanding, edge detection and morphological algorithms.

Another task undertaken by the DVP 100 is automatic foreground video manipulation. Virtual set designers that incorporate an element such as a light source can also design the effect this light source will have on foreground elements. For example, if there is a flashing red light in the virtual environment, the DVP will automatically paint the foreground objects, showing the effect of the flashing red light on these objects. There is no need of using actual physical red lighting for this effect as the DVP automatically manipulates the video for the lighting effect.

Foreground video manipulation can also be used in real-time for high/low pass filtering and can even change the color of a presenter's clothing. This means that if the presenter arrives at the studio in green clothing and the producer prefers that they are wearing a different color, the DVP is implemented to change the color of the clothing. The DVP can even be used to remove wrinkles on the presenter's face.

Lastly, the processor can sharpen the video in the foreground areas by generating a detailed foreground image without chroma-key artifacts.

❖ **CyberCamera**—An innovated technique that enables performance of virtual dolly movements of the camera, that extend beyond the studio's physical boundaries, while keeping all the real objects in the field of view. The CyberCamera effect is based on live manipulation and composition of the foreground video with the virtual background,

❖ **MobileSet**—A unique concept in virtual set technology that allows the insertion of virtual scenes, animation and video sequences into live outside broadcasts. Set up and deployed in minutes, MobileSet can easily be set up by a single operator. It is ideal for any outside event: sports events, outdoor concerts and festivals, and commercial and on-the-spot location news reports.

❖ **CyberShadow**—A virtual shadow for objects and actors in the blue space, added directly and in real-time to the 3-D model. The virtual shadow can be manipulated, animated and switched on and off at any time.

❖ **Virtual Reflection editor (optional)**—Virtual reflections of real objects can be presented in the image using a proprietary technology. The reflection intensity and its spatial distribution can be change in real time. Virtual reflection is definitely the best way to create a photo-realistic illusion in a virtual set.

❖ **RealSet**—is designed to allow the seamless integration of virtual objects, such as 3-D graphics and virtual characters into conventional studio productions in real-time. RealSet can also be used to modify real objects by changing their color and even adding virtual lighting with realistic shadowing to enhance the mood of a conventional production.

❖ **Improved video delay factor**—ORAD has paid much attention to users' concerns of the video delay factor in virtual productions. The result is a marked improvement in CyberSet's video delay factor being narrowed down to as low as 1 to 3 video frames depending on the operation mode.

❖ **An improved user friendly user interface**—ORAD has introduced a new user interface for CyberSet (Version 3.1) which offers the professional and nontechnical user alike, ease of use and greater control without compromising the product's openness and flexibility. The new interface has been designed to reflect the way studio technicians work in the real world. Ostensibly, ORAD has translated what is a complicated environment into one that is now more intuitive and easier to master.

The user interface contains such helpful features as a troubleshooting module that guides the user through all the modules of CyberSet to ensure a smoothly and correctly running system. Studio settings can be saved as files for effortless retrieval.

Also, a wide variety of CyberSet functions are now accessible directly on the control screen making the system's operation more understandable for the nontechnical user to execute.

❖ **Widescreen capabilities**—With the growing demand by broadcasters for productions to be produced in the widescreen format (16:9), ORAD now offers this capability across the full-range of CyberSets.

❖ **Software loader for Softimage designed sets**—ORAD has developed an improved software loader designed to allow the import of Softimage models and animations for use in conjunction with the company's CyberSet virtual studio. CyberSet users can now harness the creative power of Softimage's modeling and animation tools to create totally believable virtual elements and environments for virtual set productions.

❖ **Multipanel operations**—CyberSet can now work with several panels on several walls. 270/360 degrees shooting capability is thus obtained.

❖ The graphical **rendering power** of the SGI Onyx has been enhanced using an ORAD's proprietary technology. For example, a 2xRM7 Onyx system can have the performance of a 4xRM7 machine. This is a free upgrade to CyberSet users.

❖ **A Virtual Camera** is a feature that enables you to present the set from every desired perspective. It can be used to capture areas of the scene that are far beyond the real studio boundaries. Virtual camera shots can be seamlessly integrated with real camera ones. The virtual camera gives the possibility of showing various points of view, thus, for example, the set can be seen from the real character's point of view.

❖ Background image areas may be "protected" (not replaced with foreground in non-blue zones) using a **"garbage matte."** The boundaries of the blue studio may thus be greatly extended.

❖ **External devices**, such as computer running statistical, games or scoring programs, may be interfaced with CyberSet computer to allow real-time interactive update of data. Election results may thus be automatically injected and updated and interactive TV games may be played in the virtual set.

❖ **An Audio/Video management module** is offered as an option to CyberSet users. This module serves to control the various audio and video signals in case of an interview between a local presenter (located in the virtual set) and a remote correspondent, so that the audio delay on the virtual set display will fit the video delay and the transition between the virtual set and the remote video feed will be smooth.

❖ **Various sound effects** may be added and combined with predesigned animations.

❖ **Any number of video windows** may be inserted into a set. The video can be wrapped on any virtual object. The system can get two independent full resolution video inputs.

❖ The foreground video may be geometrically manipulated in real-time so that the real actors are moved or rotated in space.

❖ CyberSet system supports Silicon Graphics Onyx2 Reality Engine and IR, Octane and O2 lines of products.

❖ ORAD offers a variety of CyberSet configurations addressing preview, backup for live production and video effects requirements.

Novel Cyberset Features:

Integration of sensor-based cameras into Cyberset:

One of CyberSets main advantage is the ability and flexibility to use any combination of pattern-recognition based cameras with tracking head based cameras, to have the creativity and capabilities desired by buyer.

ORAD has developed superior tracking heads with pan mode resolution capabilities of 1 million pulses in 360 degrees and with tilt mode resolution capabilities of 1.4 million pulses in 360 degrees!

Customer can choose any combination of pattern recognition and tracking head modes. ORAD integrates its pattern-recognition based virtual set with its own developed tracking heads or with any other commercially available tracking head, such as Thoma and Radamec.

As a one-stop technology shop, ORAD provides a powerful functionality no other virtual set provider can offer:

❖ Any mix of pattern recognition/sensor-based cameras.

❖ Use any given camera first in a sensor mode and then instantly dolly it in a pattern recognition mode.

❖ Use the sensor-based camera in a sensor mode, change to a new position in the studio when "off-air" and instantly recalibrate the position in the new location using ORAD's grid. ORAD's back-wall pattern is then used for automatic/immediate recalibration of a sensor-based camera in a new position.

Integration of infra-red camera tracking system into Cyberset:

ORAD's novel camera tracking system **InfraTrack** is used to measure both position and orientation of the studio camera enabling a 360 degree shooting sector. InfraTrack allows for unrestricted camera movement in a blue studio as well as in real-set environments, indoors and outdoors. ORAD's experience in the development of unique Electro-optical proprietary technology has led to the development of specially positioned LEDs. These camera-mounted LEDs enable accurate measuring of all camera parameters. Each LED is given a unique identification, which greatly enhances the ability to track the LEDs, even in extreme conditions, such as abrupt camera movements or sharp tilt angles. The new device, based on infrared detection technology, compliments ORAD's line of pattern recognition and encoder based trackers. ORAD's InfraTrack system can be mounted on any type of camera, including handheld and Steadicam. Combing the InfraTrack system with ORAD's proprietary grid calibration enables easy installation, allowing users to begin working almost immediately.

The InfraTrack system supports all of CyberSet's features, which are based on ORAD's extensive experience and technical know-how.

Infrared detection technology:
ORAD is using infrared detection technology (IR beacons on objects, directional receivers on the Studio ceiling) for automatic location of moving real objects in the studio, like cameras, actors and other objects onto which a computer generated objects need to be attached.

The infrared detection modules are used for automatic depth-keying and additional capabilities and precision.

ORAD's IR tracking system can handles up to four overhead IR cameras at once, making it possible for Studio cameras and actors to move freely within the blue space and be continuously identified.

Motion capture:
The main advantages of ORAD's Motion Capture option are the following:

❖ It interfaces with CyberSet so that motion-captured characters can be integrated into the virtual set using a single rendering platform (one Onyx).

❖ The fact above allows a common depth key for all virtual and real objects in the set, including the motion captured characters.

❖ This is the only system that is "Royalty free." Competitors charge money for each single character that a buyer would like to buy. ORAD, on the other hand, offers its buyers to buy a performance animation system with no additional charges for characters. Customers can create as many characters as they want!

❖ Extremely short calibration period—with our system a full body calibration period is one second! Average calibration periods for competing systems are between 10 min to 3 hours!

❖ Special effects—we have special effects like smoke, explosions, ripple, rubber.

❖ Multiple characters—powerful rendering enables multiple characters to perform and interact on the same computer.

❖ The system is optimized for all Silicon Graphics workstations. Minimum requirement is O2 64 MB.

❖ The system interfaces any controlling device (data gloves, facial capture, spacemouse, etc.)

The hardware consists of an electromagnetic transmitter, full body motion capture sensors and suit (11 receivers), a glove, harness and a control/processing computer (there is also a wireless version). Buyer needs to provide an SGI O2 workstation.

The software consists of a Typhoon Motion Capture and CyberSet Interface and Processing code for integration of Mocap characters.

The Motion Capture option can be used in conjunction with CyberSet and also as a standalone application in a real studio.

Studio concept:
A seamless studio integration concept and automatic preview generation for all cameramen. You use your studio switcher and CYBERSET automatically knows your on-air selection and routes the correct channel to the SGI, with the other channels going into ORAD's preview generator.

ORAD's CYBERSET configuration also addresses backup requirements for live productions, and provide capabilities for video effects, such as fade and wipe between two cameras.

Digital enhancement of the foreground video:
Using ORAD's DVP-100 Digital Video Processor you carry out any digital enhancement function on the foreground video without any penalty. This way you can sharpen your image without the usual associated chroma-key artifacts. Additional real-time video processing functions under development are color correction and manipulation, skin color adjustment, gamma correction, image stabilization and more.

CyberSet E™
CyberSet makes virtual studio sets affordable for every studio. As an entry level system, CyberSet E™ delivers the basic functionality you need to begin to reap the rewards of virtual productions.

The secret is ORAD's unique pattern recognition technology, which is based on the video itself and has no physical connection to the cameras. CyberSet E does away with the need for cumbersome studio installations, uncomfortable memory heads and clumsy robotic cameras. Camera position, orientation and lens zoom are extracted in real-time by CyberSet E, using the video itself.

Any type and model of studio lens can be used. No drift, warm-up, backlash or other mechanical problems exit. Absolutely no calibration is required. Hand-held, Steadicams or even shoulder-mounted cameras may be used. Best of all, one CyberSet E system serves any number of studio cameras.

The same studio can be used for consecutive virtual and conventional productions. Multiple studios can be connected to the same CyberSet system. Maintenance is simple and very economical. Installation and system preparation are easy and straightforward—no cumbersome, time-consuming calibration and set-up.

On non-live shows, the flexibility of CyberSet E, coupled with the power of the SGI O2 rendering platform, provides the ability to produce unlimited quality and complexity of graphical sets. The system performs frame-by-frame high quality rendering, using the camera's recorded positions/orientation data. The prerendering process is powerful and quick, such that even a daily change of program backgrounds or additional camera locations are available.

CyberSet E is fully upgradable to the high end CyberSet O™, the unquestionable leader in virtual sets. Customer's original investment is fully protected because CyberSet E is a sub-set of CyberSet O, featuring the same proven software and Digital Video Processing hardware. The migration path is built-in. The upgrade to CyberSet O is easy, swift and affordable.

ORAD also offers a sensor-based entry-level virtual set solution, CYBER-SET™, based on ORAD's own made Vinten Vision 30 and Vector 70 sensorized pan and tilt units. The main advantage over equivalent sensor-based virtual set solutions is that, by using a small off-studio coded panel and a DVP-50 unit, the studio cameras can change location while off-air, immediately calibrate their position using the grid and be ready to go on-air in their new position. CYBERSET E can also interface to other sensorized pan and tilt units like Thoma and Radamec.

Cyberset E can operate in three different modes:

2-D

❖ High resolution still images from any conventional 2-D or 3-D graphics software

❖ Free camera motion (including dolly)

❖ Multiple live video windows:

   Two full resolution inputs

   Replicated content

   Multiple content using external picture-in-picture device

❖ Full video background

❖ Masking of still images

   Foreground occlusion

   Video insertion masking

Prerendered 3-D

This mode enables the generation of superior 3-D graphical quality, unlimited by the rendering platform.

❖ Predefined camera positions

❖ Free pan-tilt-roll-zoom motions

❖ Rapid and flexible offline rendering

❖ Switches between cameras are automatically synchronized with the 3-D backgrounds

❖ Unlimited 3-D scene complexity and richness

❖ Rendering process can be done using popular software, including Alias, Softimage and Lightscape

❖ Multiple live video insertions from two full-resolution video inputs plus video reflections

❖ Animation of the video windows

❖ Enhanced texture animation for prerendered animated backgrounds

❖ 4K x 4K texture size

Full 3-D

❖ Full camera motion, including dolly, up-down and pan-tilt-roll-zoom

❖ Real-time rendering, at 50 or 60 Hz, of a basic virtual environment

❖ Handles simple 3-D objects

❖ The use of real objects will enable set modeling optimization

CyberSet E—Basic Configuration

The following table lists the hardware and software items of which CyberSet E is built:

Hardware Modules

Hardware items supplied by ORAD:

	UNIT	QTY.	DESCRIPTION
1.	Wall Patterned Grid	1	The grid is composed of two shades of blue for pattern recognition—designed and prepared by ORAD according to studio plan.
2.	DVP – 50	1	The video processor is used to extract the camera position, orientation and zoom parameters, all in real-time.
3.	DVI	1	Insert unique ID signal for each camera.

Hardware items supplied by buyer:

	UNIT	QTY.	DESCRIPTION
1.	SGI O2 Workstation	1	Utilized for graphical rendering and user interface.
2.	Studio Cameras	Unlimited no. of cameras	Ordinary camera/lens systems with their original pan/tilt units, tripods and dollies. Steadicams, handheld or shoulder mounted cameras may be used. A single CyberSet system supports any number of cameras!
3.	Switcher/Mixer	1	In order to select the camera that goes on air.

	UNIT	QTY.	DESCRIPTION
4.	Lighting	1	Standard studio lighting.
5.	Chroma-Keyer (*)	1	Chroma-keyer to composite the foreground and background video signals.

(*) No need for this unit if buyer already has a switcher with a chroma-keyer built-in.

(**) ORAD provides full set of guidelines and instructions for studio preparation.

Software Modules (Supplied by ORAD)

1) DVP real-time pattern recognition code.

2) SGI embedded set-up and run-time user interface modules.

3) Rendering and visualization module for the SGI workstation.

As mentioned above, CyberSet E basic configuration can provide a complete studio solution and serve any number of cameras in the studio. If additional cameras are added to the studio, no additional cost is incurred.

Silicon Graphics Workstation Configuration:

The following configuration of the SGI O2 workstation is recommended:

❖ 200 MHz R5000SC

❖ 128 MB, 2 GB disk

❖ 1,280 × 1,024, 17" monitor

❖ Videoboard

DVP-50 Main Specifications:

Performance:	15 Giga operations per second
Features:	Multi-MVP parallel architecture
	Compatible with PAL and NTSC standards
Data interface:	Standard parallel port
Video input/output:	Serial Digital (SDI) or Parallel Digital
Physical specs:	Height—15 $^3/_4$ in.
	Width—18 $^3/_4$ in.
	Depth—16 $^5/_8$ in.
	Weight—40 lbs.

Environmental:	Meets FCC and CE-MARKS standards
Nonoperating temperature:	-10 to 60° (at sea level)
Operating temperature:	10 to 35° (at sea level)
Heat dissipation:	2,500 btu/hr (max.)
Electrical specifications:	Power: 90-132 / 180-264 VAC, 380W max.
	Frequency: 47 to 500 Hz

Cyberset M/O—Basic Configuration

ORAD's CyberSet M product is based on SGI's Onyx2 Reality (as opposed to CyberSet O which is based on Onyx2 Infinite Reality).

Cyberset M has high quality anti-aliasing (same quality as O) and can handle large number of polygons—enough to make non-trivial 3-D sets. The number of polygons in Cyberset M (geometry processing) is half that of Cyberset O.

Cyberset M supports all modes of camera tracking, as well as, all graphics/video feature-set of Cyberset O, such as:

❖ video on 3-D objects

❖ garbage key, depth key, animation, transparencies, reflection mapping

It also supports all texture modes of Cyberset O (32-bit RGBA, tri-linear filtering, etc.) and has same amount of texture memory as Cyberset O (64 MB).

The usual configuration is with a single Raster Manager (RM) board. And, due to a special rendering technique developed by ORAD, the rasterization (rasterization is the filling of polygons, with texture and color, and depth-ordering) power of Cyberset M with a single raster manager (RM) is equivalent to two raster managers. The effective power of two RMs is equivalent to four.

The complexity of a set depends both on the number of polygons, lights (geometry) and on the total number of rendered pixels (rasterization). The second can be larger than the area of the video frame since different objects may lie behind each other. The amount of "polygon overlap" is called "depth complexity." Depth complexity of 3.5, for example, means that each pixel is covered by 3.5 polygons on an average. For that reason, sets with fairly large depth complexity, even with transparencies, can be rendered in real-time (depth complexity—approx. 4)

Cyberset M supports anti-aliasing together with key generation (garbage and depth).

This is achieved by a special technique developed in ORAD specifically for it (it is needed because normal operation of Onyx2 Reality does not support pixels with both anti-aliasing and alpha).

The basic CyberSet O configuration comprises of ORAD's proprietary video processing engine (DVP-100), a Silicon Graphics Onyx 2 IR workstation, a Silicon Graphics O2 workstation for user interface and real-time animation, automatic depth-key and camera tracking module, a coded wall pattern and standard studio equipment including ordinary studio cameras, switcher/router and a chroma-keyer. In addition, it includes the licenses to use the software packages for the CyberSet O application.

The "pixel level" depth-key module is offered as part of the system's basic configuration. It is composed of two ceiling-mounted (low-quality) TV cameras, a Silicon graphics O2 workstation and a software license.

Hardware Modules

The Silicon Graphics workstations can be directly purchased by buyer or purchased and delivered by ORAD. ORAD is SGI Value Added Reseller and may thus sometimes propose better prices than local SGI dealers.

Hardware items supplied by ORAD:

	UNIT	QTY	DESCRIPTION
1.	Wall Patterned Grid	1	The grid is composed of two shades of blue for pattern recognition tasks. This pattern is designed and prepared by ORAD according to the studio plan.
2.	DVP-100	1	The video processor is used to extract the camera position, orientation and zoom parameters, all in real-time.
3.	DVI	1	The video processor is used to extract the camera position, orientation and zoom parameters, all in real-time.
4.	The automatic depth-key/camera tracking module	1	For automatic location of moving real objects in the studio, like cameras, actors and other objects.
5.	SGI Onyx 2 IR or SGI Onyx 2 Reality	1 1	For Cyberset O For Cyberset M

	UNIT	QTY.	DESCRIPTION
6.	SGI O2 Workstation	3	For the automatic depth-key and tracking of infrared LEDs in a given 3-D space.
7.	SGI O2 Workstation	1	Utilized for graphical rendering and Animation User Interface.

Hardware items supplied by buyer:

	UNIT	QTY.	DESCRIPTION
1.	Studio Cameras	Unlimited number of cameras	Ordinary camera/lens systems with their original pan/tilt units, tripods and dollies. Steadicams, handheld or shoulder mounted cameras may be used. A single CyberSet system supports any number of cameras!
2.	Switcher/Mixer	1	In order to select the camera that goes on-air. In case of an analog switcher, a digital converter should be connected to the switcher.
3.	Lighting	1	Standard studio lighting.
4.	Chroma-Keyer*	1	Chroma-keyer to composite the foreground and background video signals.

* No need for this unit if buyer already has a switcher with a chroma-keyer built-in.

** ORAD provides full guidelines and instructions for studio preparation.

Software Modules (Supplied by ORAD):

❖ DVP real-time pattern recognition code.

❖ SGI embedded set-up and real-time user interface modules.

❖ MultiGen module for 3-D set and models design and for real-time preparation.

❖ Rendering and visualization module for the SGI workstation.

❖ Real-time animation user interface.

❖ Automatic depth-key/camera tracking module.

As mentioned above, the Cyberset M/O basic configuration can provide a complete studio solution and serves any number of cameras in the studio. If more cameras are added to the studio, no additional cost in incurred.

ORAD is proud to offer a new system concept enabling a preview video feed of the composited image to each cameraman all the time.

Realization of this feature requires a proprietary device ("Preview Generator") supplied by ORAD and a Silicon Graphics O-2 workstation for each preview channel.

Silicon Graphics Workstations Configurations

SGI Onyx

Cyberset supports ANY configuration of Silicon Graphics Reality Engine2 and Infinite Reality Onyx1 as well as Onyx2 workstations. Cyberset can use a single CPU Onyx machine.

Typical recommended Onyx 2 IR configuration for Cyberset O

❖ 2 x R10000 CPUs, 256 MB RAM

❖ 4.5 GB disk, 2 x RM8 (64 MB)

❖ DIVO in/out + GVO

Typical recommended Onyx 2 Reality configuration for Cyberset M

❖ 1 x R10000 CPUs, 256 MB RAM

❖ 4.5 GB disk, 1 x RM8 (64 MB)

❖ DIVO in/out + GVO

User interface O2:

❖ R 5000 SC

❖ 180/200 MHz, 128 MB RAM, 4 GB disk

Automatic Depth-key O2 Workstations (X2):

❖ R 5000 SC, 2 GB disk

❖ 200 MHz, 64 MB RAM, Video option

DVP-100 Main Specifications:

Performance:	15 to 30 Giga operations per second
Features:	Multi-MVP parallel architecture
	Compatible with PAL and NTSC standards
Data interface:	Standard parallel port
Video input/output:	Serial Digital (SDI) or Parallel Digital
Physical specs:	Height—15 $^3/_4$ in.
	Width—18 $^3/_4$ in.

Depth—16 $^5/_8$ in.

Weight—40 lbs.

Environmental: Meets FCC and CE-MARKS standards

Non operating temperature: –10° to 60°
  (at sea level)

Operating temperature: 10° to 35° (at sea level)

Heat dissipation: 2,500 btu/hr (max)

Electrical specs: Power: 90-132 / 180-264 VAC, 380W max

Frequency: 47 to 500 Hz

CyberSet-HD

Introduction

In line with the recent developments in digital television broadcasting technology, ORAD was the first to develop a virtual studio system suitable for high-definition technology. High definition digital technology enables a much clearer image, giving viewers an ultra-realistic picture.

ORAD's CyberSetHD is a virtual-set system whereby live video of presenters operating in a blue set are seamlessly integrated with three-dimensional computer generated scenes. Any number of ordinary studio cameras may be used and the cameras can be freely moved. Camera parameters are extracted in real-time using the video itself and not by means of opto-mechanical camera-mounted sensors, like in former-generation virtual set systems. One or more sensors-based cameras may nevertheless be integrated in CyberSetHD.

CyberSetHD is used by a rapidly growing number of buyers for live broadcasting and postproduction applications. It is already "field" tested and proven in real production environments.

The modeling of the graphical sets, assignment of texture maps to objects, lighting design and animation of computer generated objects can be done using MultiGen tools that are bundled with CyberSetHD software. They can also be prepared by means of any popular commercial 3-D modeling software like Softimage 3-D, Alias Power Animator, Wavefront and others. CyberSetHD code needs only to know where the model database is stored and the format.

Using CyberSetHD production tools the operator may easily create or change entire program sets, object models, special effects and animations prior or even during the live production.

CyberSetHD removes the expenses which regular studios find when converting to the high definition format, with CyberSetHD there is no need to repair or improve physical scenery and backdrops, high resolution images are achieved instantly at the push of a button. Moreover, any existing set model can be easily upgraded to the high definition format. Any one of ORAD's products can be incorporated into the high definition system. For example, Virtual Replay models can be integrated into this system, enabling the presenter to walk between a 3-D model of a sporting event highlight.

Merits of the Pattern-Recognition Approach:

❖ ORAD's CyberSetHD is the only virtual set based on pattern recognition. Ordinary studio cameras and mounting units may thus be used.

❖ Camera position parameters are extracted in addition to orientation and zoom. Camera motion is thus unrestricted. Handheld, Steadicam, remote control cameras or even shoulder-mounted cameras may be used. No studio installation is needed; no memory heads or robotic cameras are required. Cameramen routine is not changed. The same studio used for CyberSetHD may also be utilized as a regular studio running ordinary programs, saving you space, time and money.

❖ One CyberSetHD system, with just one SGI Onyx, can serve any number of studio cameras or even several (and remote) studios.

❖ There are no calibration procedures, warm-up or backlash problems, which are associated with the sensor-based system. CyberSetHD also has greater stability and better accuracy.

❖ There is no need for special lens calibration as with other virtual set systems. The calibration of lens aberrations is done automatically using ORAD's pattern recognition engine. Every type of studio lens may be used, in opposition to other systems that impose restriction on lens type and model.

❖ CyberSetHD serves all studio cameras, buyers are not forced to buy expensive crane systems or robotic cameras, thus system costs substantially lower.

❖ The resulting maintenance costs are equally low.

❖ Installation and operation are simpler and easier; outdoor and mobile studios can be easily constructed.

CyberSet HD's Features:

CyberSetHD is not just the only virtual set based on pattern recognition. It is the most advanced system in the market as reflected by many other aspects:

❖ CyberSetHD uses a unique "pixel-level" Depth-Key module.

❖ The Virtual Presence module is offered as a free upgrade to CyberSetHD users.

❖ Depth of focus.

❖ Real shadows of real objects are reconstructed on the composite image.

❖ CyberShadows (optional)—virtual shadows of real objects can be generated using a proprietary electro-optical method and the DVP-100.

❖ Virtual Reflection editor (optional)—Virtual reflections of real objects can be presented in the image using a proprietary technology. The reflection intensity and its spatial distribution can be changed in real time. Virtual reflection is definitely the best way to create a photo-realistic illusion in a virtual set.

❖ A Virtual Camera is a feature that enables you to present the set from every desired perspective.

❖ Delay Factor—CyberSetHD's video delay factor is four video frames, depending on operational mode.

❖ RealSet—Real-time Virtual Object Insertion (optional). RealSet allows the seamless integration of virtual objects, such as 3-D graphics and virtual characters into traditional studio production in real-time.

❖ Wide Screen Capabilities—With the growing demand by broadcasters for productions to be produced in the wide screen format (16:9).

❖ Softimage Loader—ORAD's new software loader allows the import of Softimage models and animations for use in conjunction with the company's CyberSet virtual studio.

❖ Background image areas may be "protected" using a "garbage matte."

❖ External devices, such as computer running statistical, games or scoring programs, may be interfaced with CyberSetHD computer to allow real-time interactive update of data. Election results may thus be automatically injected and updated and interactive TV games may be played in the virtual set.

❖ CyberActors can be integrated using real-time motion capture.

❖ Multipanel operations CyberSet can now work with several panels on several walls. 270/360 degrees shooting capability is thus obtained.

❖ An Audio/Video management module is offered as an option.

❖ Various sound effects may be added and combined with predesigned animations or with the activation of certain degrees of freedom.

❖ Any number of video windows may be inserted into a set. The video can be wrapped on any virtual object.

❖ The foreground video may be geometrically manipulated in real-time so that the real actors are moved or rotated in space.

❖ ORAD offers a variety of CyberSetHD configurations addressing preview backup for live production and video effects requirements.

❖ CyberSetHD uses a very powerful and intuitive graphical user interface with clean and uncluttered screen and icon representations.

Novel CyberSet HD Features:

A. Interaction of sensor-based cameras into Cyberset HD:

One of CyberSetHDs main advantage is the ability and flexibility to use any combination of pattern-recognition based cameras with tracking head based cameras, to have the creativity and capabilities desired by buyer. ORAD has developed superior tracking heads with pan mode resolution capabilities of 1.5 million pulses in 360 degrees and with tilt mode resolution capabilities of 1.1 million pulses in 360 degrees. Buyer can choose any combination of pattern recognition and tracking head modes. ORAD integrates its pattern-recognition based virtual set with its own developed tracking heads or with any other commercially available tracking head.

B. Infrared detection technology:

ORAD uses infrared detection technology (IR beacons on objects, directional receivers on the upper grid) for automatic location of moving real objects in the studio, like cameras, actors and other objects onto which computer generated objects need to be attached. The infrared detection modules are used for automatic depth-keying and additional capabilities and precision.

C. Studio concept:

A seamless studio integration concept and automatic preview generation for all cameramen. You use your studio switcher and CyberSetHD automatically knows your on-air selection and routes the correct channel to the Onyx, with the other channels going into ORAD's preview generator. ORAD's CyberSetHD configuration also addresses backup requirements for live productions, and provide capabilities for video effects, such as fade and wipe between two cameras.

CyberSet HD system configurations:
The basic CyberSetHD configuration comprises ORAD's proprietary video processing engine (DVP-100), a Silicon Graphics Onyx2 Infinite Reality 2 workstation, a Silicon Graphics O2 for the user interface and real-time animation, automatic depth-key and camera tracking module, a coded wall pattern and standard studio equipment including ordinary studio cameras, switcher/-router and a chroma-keyer. In addition, it includes the licenses to use the software packages for the CyberSet HD application.

The "pixel level" depth-key module is offered as part of the system basic configuration. It is composed of two ceiling-mounted (low-quality) TV cameras, two Silicon graphics O2 workstations and a software license.

Hardware modules:
Hardware items supplied by ORAD:
- One Digital Video Processor (DVP-100) unit. These modules are used to extract in real-time the camera position, orientation and zoom parameters for the on-air and preview channels.
- A coded wall pattern composed of two shades of blue used for the pattern recognition task. This pattern is designed and prepared by ORAD according to the studio plan.
- The automatic depth-key/camera-tracking module including two overhead cameras, three camera-LED boxes, and one actor-LED module.

Supplied by buyer:
- Sony HDC-750A, or Sony HDCU-700a HDTV studio camera/lens systems with their original pan and tilt units, tripods and dollies. Steadicam or shoulder mounted cameras may be used as well. A single CyberSetHD system supports any number of cameras.
- Studio lighting according to ORAD's specs.
- Sony HDW-500 VTR.
- Sony HKPF101 and Sony HKPF102 for convertors.
- Sony HDS-7000 + Chroma-keyer switcher to composite the foreground and background video signals.
- S & W 4x HD-4000 Delay or Leitech equivalent.

Software Modules (supplied by ORAD):

❖ DVP real-time pattern recognition code.

❖ SGI embedded setup, program/set preparation and user interface modules.

❖ Softimage loader.

❖ MultiGen module for 3-D set, models design and for real-time preparation.

❖ Rendering and visualization module for the SGI workstation.

❖ Automatic depth-key/camera tracking module.

As mentioned above, the CyberSetHD basic configuration can provide a complete studio solution and serve any number of cameras in the studio. If more cameras are added to the studio, no additional cost in incurred. When a full backup system is required for live on-air productions the dual CyberSetHD configuration is recommended. In this configuration two Onyx workstations (or one Onyx with two graphical pipelines) are required.

Silicon—Graphics Workstations Configurations:
SGI Onyx:
Optimal configuration for HDTV:
Onyx2 Rack—Infinite Reality2
2 x CPU R10000
512 MB RAM, 9 GB disk
2 or 4 x RM boards 64 RAM
DIVO and HD DIVO (New Product)
User Interface SGI O2 (Qty. 1):
200 MHz R5000SC
128 MB, 4 GB disk
1,280 × 1, 024, 17" monitor

Automatic Depth-Key O2 Workstations (Qty. 2):
200 MHz 1 MB Cache R5000SC
64 MB, 4 GB disk
1,280 × 1,024, 17" monitor
Including analog video board

DVP-100 Main Specifications:

Performance: 15 to 30 Giga operations per second

Features: Multi-MVP parallel architecture

Compatible with PAL and NTSC standards

Data interface: Standard parallel port

Video input/output: Serial Digital (SDI) or Parallel Digital

Physical specs: Height—15 $^3/_4$ in.

Width—18 $^3/_4$ in.

Depth—16 $^5/_8$ in.

Weight—40 lbs.

Environmental: Meets FCC and CE-MARKS standards

Non operating temperature: $-10°$ to $60°$ (at sea level)

Operating temperature: $10°$ to $35°$ (at sea level)

Heat dissipation: 2,500 btu/hr (max)

Electrical specs: Power: 90–132/180–264 VAC, 380W max

Frequency: 47 to 500 Hz

ORAD's CyberSet Post

What is CyberSet Post?

CyberSet Post combines the advantages of ORAD's virtual set production technology with the ultimate quality results of postproduction rendering. CyberSet Post enables you to create artistic scenes where real actors interact with 3-D objects in a virtual set. With CyberSet Post you can shoot commercials, creative video clips, movie sequences as well as special effects. At the same time, it allows you to use freely moving cameras and to record their parameters without the restrictive and expensive motion control rigs.

ORAD's CyberSet is a virtual-set system whereby live video of presenters and actors operating in a blue set is seamlessly integrated with three-dimensional computer generated environments in real-time. ORAD's unique virtual set solution is based on a proven pattern recognition technology that allows for camera and lens parameters to be measured in real-time without the need for mechanical or other sensor attachments. Real-time extraction of the studio camera movements is done using a powerful image-processing engine developed by ORAD. CyberSet allows the cameraman complete freedom to use all types and any number of ordinary cameras and lenses including handheld, shoulder-mounted and Steadicam cameras, with no modification or additional cost.

Of course, real time rendering, even with the most powerful graphics engines, still has its limitations, like number of polygons, objects, lights, textures, etc. To overcome these limitations, ORAD has developed CyberSet Post.

Besides operating as a virtual set, the CyberSet Post records the parameters of the freely moving camera, together with the time code of the foreground video. Optionally, the location of the actor can be extracted and recorded as well. At the same time, real-time preview is available, in order to get an idea, on the set, of how the composed video will look like and to help actor position himself within the 3-D model.

The recorded file can be easily exported into any leading modeling and rendering tool such as Softimage/3-D, 3-D Studio Max, Lightwave, etc. Then, the off-line rendered image is combined with the foreground through easy-to-use software chroma-keying.

Benefits of CyberSet Post

CyberSet Post is ideal for creating artistic scenes where real actors interact with 3-D objects in a virtual set. With CyberSet Post you can shoot commercials, creative video clips, movie sequences as well as special effects. By rendering the virtual scenes offline, on an entry-level workstation, you can create very complex and photorealistic scenes that are not possible in high-end real-time virtual set productions.

CyberSet Post allows its users to:

❖ Use freely moving cameras while still recording their movements and parameters.

❖ Use a real-time preview to get a feedback, on the set, of how the composed video will look like.

❖ Shoot the scene again, on the spot, until the desired result is achieved.

❖ Avoid the use of restrictive and expensive motion control rigs.

❖ Make quick changes in camera positions around the studio, without spending precious time on calibration of mechanical sensor heads.

❖ Create very complex and photo-realistic scenes on an entry-level O2 workstation.

ORAD's MobileSet

MobileSet is a new product from ORAD, provider of CyberSet, the most widely used virtual set system worldwide. MobileSet allows the insertion of video and animation into live broadcasts—outdoors and indoors. ORAD's lightweight mini panel, fixed, mobile or handheld, is transformed into a virtual video screen. Using ORAD's proven pattern recognition technology, all the information needed regarding the cameras as well as the panel's position and orientation is extracted from the video feed itself. Therefore, even handheld cameras can be used freely. MobileSet is a transportable system that can easily be set up by a single operator and can be deployed in minutes.

Main Features:

❖ Insertion of video, fixed or animated 3-D objects on a small mobile panel in live indoor and outdoor broadcast.

❖ Panel size from as small as 20 cm up to several meters long.

❖ The panel can be handheld and is lightweight.

❖ Free from any attached markers or sensors.

❖ No initialization or calibration is needed.

❖ Uses any type of camera.

❖ No special add-ons are needed.

❖ Easily set up by a single operator.

Benefits of MobileSet

MobileSet is ideal for displaying video and animation, creating a controlled environment, and adding extra excitement to outdoor productions, such as live interviews, sports broadcasts, outdoor weather forecast programs, interviews, on-the-spot news reports, outdoor concerts and musical festivals. MobileSet enables its users to:

❖ Display video without the logistics that is involved with setting up big screen monitors in outdoor shootings.

❖ Avoid the limitations and quality degradation that comes with filming video screens.

❖ Interact with and refer to the inserted video and animations.

❖ Bring complete mobility and flexibility to all broadcast production.

❖ Display a virtual video wall behind the reporter in order to create a controlled and disturbance free environment in outdoor broadcasting.

❖ Display statistics, charts and other information.

❖ Add advertisements and sponsorship messages.

❖ Add visual effects to outdoor live broadcasts.

Configurations:

MobileSet is offered in two configurations:

❖ *Stand-alone MobileSet system*—a transportable system for outdoor broad-casting and indoor conventional studios. In this configuration, MobileSet cannot be used as a CyberSet virtual set.

❖ *MobileSet add-on option for CyberSet E/M/O*—the combined system can be operated either as MobileSet or as CyberSet E/M/O, respectively.

RADAMEC

RADAMEC GROUP PLC

"At the Leading Edge of Technology"

Radamec's sophisticated system engineered products enjoy strong positions in Broadcast, Television, Defense and other specialized industrial niche markets. Technical excellence, quality, reliability, service and life cycle costs are pre-eminent factors in the Radamec products supplied to international markets. The group's high quality innovative engineering design and development capabilities ensure products meet the constantly evolving requirements of the customer.

Radamec Broadcast Systems competitively priced Virtual Reality TV Studio system (named Virtual Scenario) comprises special versions of Radamec's robotic products and a new Digital Video Effects electronic system (DVE) developed by the BBC R&D department with robotic camera control equipment inputs from Radamec. This cooperation resulted in an exclusive worldwide licensing arrangement for Radamec Broadcast Systems to manufacture and sell the system.

The system allows computer generated backgrounds or live action video to be used as the "set" in studio production instead of scenery expensively built and erected inside the studio

Entry Level Virtual Scenario System Components

The video processing technology on which Virtual Scenario is based means that it is always working with standard video signals. This makes integration into a studio environment very straightforward.

435VR Pan and Tilt Head

The camera interface uses Radamec's own 435VR pan and tilt head. Essentially, this is our successful 435 standard head, but incorporates high-resolution encoders that can detect the slightest camera movement. The head has variable fluid damping to ensure optimum smooth movement in manual mode, and the remote control version also has electronically declutched motors to enable manual operation also.

Pan and tilt head specifications:

Pan Range (Remote): 350°

Pan Range (local): Unlimited

Tilt Range: ±40

Maximum Speed (remote): 60°/s
Maximum payload: 50Kgs
Repeatability: 3 mins of arc
Resolution 0.001° (with SPI)

Serial Position Interface (SPI)

The SPI is a powerful digital signal processor that is fitted onto the side of the pan and tilt head. It has visual LED indications to monitor correct operation and encoder movement over all axes. The positional information received from the head and lens is combined into a single high-speed data stream. As well as information from the pan and tilt head, the SPI will receive zoom and focus data from encoders positioned on the camera lens. These provide essential data with a resolution in excess of 10,000 samples.

Scenario Control Unit (User Workstation)

The User Workstation receives the SPI data from all cameras and passes information to the Scenario unit. It has a user friendly touch screen interface, displaying buttons which are pressed to select features, and set up the camera channels.

The workstation itself can control up to eight different camera channels, so multichannel systems do not require additional workstations. As well as the touch buttons, the display also shows a graphical representation of background positioning. Both enlarged and reduced size pictures are represented with respect to camera framing, so the operator has a reliable indication of panning area. As well as calculating and storing lens calibration information, the other main controls of the user workstation are as follows:

❖ Selection of auto or manual mode (engage or disengage).

❖ Selection of 1:1 picture size (full frame).

❖ Selection of freeze frame (picture grab).

❖ Calibrate for lens characteristics.

❖ Selection of film (frame) mode or video (field) mode.

❖ Move and change the size of the virtual image.

Most of these controls are set up functions, the two most commonly used controls, "full frame" and "engage/disengage," can be remotely accessed by the camera operator, so Virtual Scenario does not normally need a full time operator.

Virtual Scenario Unit

The Virtual Scenario Studio System unit is the central processing unit and carries out the video processing functions necessary for Virtual Studio operations. The unit consists of a 2RU chassis with slots for 3 printed circuit boards. As standard, one of these slots is taken up by the video processing board. This will take virtual set video image, then digitally process the video according to data on camera movement, simultaneously received from the user workstation. Using mathematical algorithms, the Scenario ensures that the correct perspectives are applied to the background video as the studio camera pans, tilts and zooms.

The other two spaces within the unit are for the optional key processor, and digital to analogue converter and delay boards, which are described in more detail in the Options section.

VIRTUAL SCENARIO OPTIONS

The system description above is based on an entry level Virtual Scenario. This configuration alone allows the user to commence virtual studio production. There are, however, upgrade paths available that can add realism to a set, and further ease integration of Virtual Scenario into the studio system.

A to D Converter and Delay

This is an optional board that will fit into the Virtual Scenario Main Unit, so no extra space is needed. It includes an A to D converter, if the studio cameras are analogue, signal conversion is done internally. The same board adds the required four field delay to synchronize the camera signal to the processed video.

Specifications:

A to D converter: 10 bit
Input: RGBS/YUV
Delay Module: 4 fields (adjustable)
Input/Output: 270 MHz serial digital CCIR 601
Cable Eq: To 100m

Key Channel Processor

This is also a printed circuit board that fits into the Virtual Scenario main unit. The Key Processor provides a second channel of video processing. This signal can then be used by a chroma-keyer to mask areas of the foreground, with the result that virtual objects can be placed in front of real objects. As the Key signal is processed in exactly the same way as the virtual set, it follows the virtual set movement, as the studio camera moves.

D.Focus

D.Focus is a separate video processor that enhances virtual studio realism by adding depth of field to the virtual set thus replicating the zoom and focus characteristics of a real camera lens. In a real environment, when a camera lens is focused on an object in the foreground, we would normally expect the background to be out of focus. This effect is exaggerated as the zoom length of the lens increases.

Rendering these effects convincingly in real time requires exceptional processing power, making most real time renders unable to reproduce the effects correctly.

The hardware solution used by D.Focus allows real time defocusing effects without limitations. D.Focus calculates virtual set distances by use of a depth map. The Depth Map is a monochrome image of the set similar to a conventional matte. In the case of a depth map, white areas indicate objects that are near to the camera position and dark areas indicate objects that are further away. The depth map itself can either be created by the same graphics system that created the set, or painted manually.

While the depth map is fed into an input on the D.Focus unit, the virtual set is defocused in response to feedback from the lens sensors. The resulting image is then supplied to Virtual Scenario in the usual way for zoom, pan and tilt manipulation.

Virtual Scenario V3-D (VIRTUAL 3-D)

As discussed earlier, many virtual studio productions do not necessarily need on-air 3-D camera movements. However, in some cases the facility to be able to move the camera in three dimensions may be desirable.

Virtual 3-D (V3-D), a powerful new development for the Virtual Scenario system, combines all the advantages and simplicity of a 2-D virtual studio yet allows a useful range of camera movement in three dimensions (i.e. pan, tilt, zoom, focus, X, Y, Z and roll).

The 2-D virtual set is positioned in "3-D space" by simple touch screen entry of dimensions from the approximate studio camera position. This setup is done only once at the beginning of a show and requires no further intervention during transmission. The V3-D system then takes care of moving the set in three dimensions according to the precisely sensed camera movements. 3-D parallax effects between virtual background and real foreground are correctly recreated as the V3-D system understands that the virtual set is at a certain distance from the camera and must therefore move at a certain speed when the camera moves across the floor.

The very natural appearance of this parallax effect convinces the eye that the two dimensional virtual set image is in fact three dimensional. This illusion is convincing over a surprisingly wide area of camera movement, enabling significant re-positioning of the studio camera while on-air—something that has never previously been possible on a 2-D system.

The result of this enhancement is a very cost effective, reliable, and realistic virtual set system that can support all axes of camera movements (even roll when used with a suitable sensing system). The advantages of prerendered graphics and high quality video processing still apply, enabling virtual 3-D sets to be of a quality unequalled by expensive real-time rendering computer based 3-D systems.

RP2VR

When moving the camera through three-dimensional space, the demands on sensor equipment are even higher than when moving the camera from a static base. Radamec manufactures sensor systems to meet these demands and can supply a system to meet every application and budget.

If robotic control is required, the RP2VR remote controlled pedestal will not only provide full remote movement of the camera, but built-in VR sensors will accurately sense every movement over the three axes. On board the RP2 pedestal is a sophisticated optical navigational system. This system references itself to bar code targets attached to the back of the studio wall, which allow the RP2 to calculate the precise position and movement. No navigational aids such as tape or homing plates are required. If the RP2's view of the targets become obscured, it will automatically switch to "dead reckoning" mode where it will take measurements as it moves. It will subsequently re-reference itself to the studio targets when they come back into view. Although the RP2 has been primarily designed for remote control use, it can easily be switched to manual operation.

Free-d Tracking

If fully manual or even handheld camera control is required, then the Free-d sensor system is an ideal solution. This uses a small CCD camera mounted onto the studio based camera, the CCD camera has a ring of LEDs around the lens which illuminate uniquely identifiable markers on the studio ceiling, the resulting image is fed to the Free-d processor unit. From the CCD camera's image of the targets, the processor can identify the exact position of the studio camera on the studio floor and can identify any movement and pan and tilt change. The Free-d camera is unobtrusive enough to allow handheld camera operation.

RT-SET

RT-SET (Real Time Synthesized Entertainment Technology) Ltd., headquartered in New York, is a leading provider of fully integrated broadcast graphics solutions including highly sophisticated, easy-to-use Virtual Studio Systems, comprehensive on-air graphics packages and character generator systems, creative design services and real-time 3-D data visualization.

RT-SET's vision is to become the acknowledged leader in increasing customer productivity and profitability in the broadcasting market with high quality, integrated digital solutions and creative services.

RT-SET presently develops, markets and integrates highly sophisticated, easy-to-use Virtual Studio Systems and comprehensive broadcast graphics packages primarily for television stations, production houses and special events.

RT-SET offers a wide range of products and services that can be offered as integrated turnkey solutions, including the following elements.

RT-SET Creative Services offer unparalleled experience in the creation of virtual sets, real-time broadcast graphics and data display. Services offered include a complete Sets Library, Customized Applications and Consulting Services.

Users, including leading global players in the broadcasting, entertainment and production industries, currently enjoy RT-SET systems in a variety of daily and special productions including news, elections, magazines, sports, weather, children's programming, educational programs, documentaries, special events, corporate communications and more.

RT-SET offers its clients turnkey solutions and takes complete responsibility for studio and systems integration, including hardware and software, installation, training and ongoing support.

Ibis Product Description:

Ibis is a fully integrated, entry level virtual studio system providing realistic, 3-D effects for television stations and production houses.

RT-SET's Ibis is an economical, yet sophisticated plug-and-play Virtual Studio System providing realistic 3-D effects. The system requires minimal installation and no special training is necessary, due to its ease of use. Due to its unique, very high-resolution background capability, Ibis is the most flexible and realistic low cost virtual studio system available today. It is especially useful for programs such as news, magazines and sport coverage. The system enables the user to operate a virtual studio without restrictions on the camera movements. It accepts very high-resolution background images in a variety of formats (tiff, jpeg, rgb, pic, etc.), from any standard image manipulation program (PhotoShop, PhotoPaint, etc.). The background image can be much larger than the displayed video (4,096 × 4,096 pixels), enabling a wide range of pan, tilt and zoom movements without the loss of the fine details in the background image. Ibis includes an intuitive and self-explanatory user interface, which combines all functions into one window. Ibis can operate in conjunction with RT-SET's Larus, or be upgraded to Larus at any time.

Ibis features:
❖ Foreground /background images and obstructions.

❖ Any cyclorama shape.

❖ Unlimited number of cameras.

❖ Multilanguage user interface support.

❖ Automatic trash matte.

❖ Supports unlimited pan, tilt, zoom and focus.

❖ Preproduction tools.

❖ Video window with wipes and DVE effects.

❖ Simultaneous support of multiple sets.

❖ Enables both flat and cylindrical backgrounds.

❖ Simultaneous support of two different, full resolution video inputs.

❖ Perspective view of video windows.

❖ Plug-in support for interface to external devices.

❖ Instant switch between backgrounds.

Graphics computer:
SGI O2 R5000 – 200 MHz CPU
256 MB RAM
4 GB Hard Disk
Update rate: 50 Hz/60 Hz
Graphic formats: Kodak PhotoCD overview (PCDO); SOFTIMAGE image (SOFTIMAGE); NITF image (NITF); USGS DOQ (DOQ); Windows bitmap

image (BMP); FIT image (FIT); Classic SGI image (SGI); JFIF/JPEG image (JFIF); Raw image (Raw); TIFF image (TIFF); PNG image (PNG); PPM image (PNG); PPM image (PPM); XPM image (XPM); YUV image (YUV); Alias image (Alias); XBM image (XBM); GIF image (GIF); Kodak PhotoCD image (PCD).

Keyers: Analog/Digital

Switchers: Analog/Digital

Video standards: PAL/NTSC/16:9/SECAM

Video inputs: two full resolution

Tracking systems
- ❖ Thoma tracking systems
- ❖ Vinten TSM
- ❖ Radamec
- ❖ BBC's FreeD
- ❖ Mark Roberts Milo
- ❖ Thoma WolkFinder
- ❖ Xync, X-Pecto
- ❖ Hawkeye
- ❖ Crane
- ❖ Dolly and more

LARUS Product Description
General

RT-SET's Larus Virtual Studio System provides a comprehensive solution for all stages of TV program production. Being a fully integrated system, all cameras, tracking systems, computers and control units are connected to and operate with the virtual world and the control room simultaneously. One operator alone can manage and control the entire system. The Larus is an "open system" which allows users to easily defines studio configurations or create sets and lineups using standard modelers, during any stage of the production.

Larus Features

In addition to integrating live actors with 3-D virtual sets in real time, RT-SET has developed unique features which make productions fast and easy, and provide almost unlimited flexibility for the creative staff:

❖ Unlimited number of cameras.

❖ Unrestrained camera movements including handheld.

❖ Any kind of obstruction.

❖ Switching and dissolve between cameras and between sets.

❖ Online Video Cursor.

❖ Video Clips.

❖ 3-D Sound Effects.

❖ Manipulations of live talent with 3-D effects.

❖ Control of Out-of-Focus and Depth of Field.

❖ Automatic Trash Matte.

❖ Virtual Camera.

❖ Virtual Switcher.

❖ Plug in to external systems.

❖ Template Graphic Support.

❖ Preproduction Tools.

❖ Studio to Virtual Mapping Tool.

❖ Postproduction Tools.

❖ Backup and Preview System (O2 based).

❖ Enchore Prompter.

❖ Virtual Shadow.

❖ Lighting Effects.

System Specifications:
Graphics Computer:
SGI Onyx RE/IR
Onyx2 Reality IR/IR2
2 CPU R 10,000
4 GB Disk
RM6, 64 MB Texture Memory (2 recommended)

256 MB RAM
2 GB DAT
DIVO
GVO
Async Comm. Board

Control Station: (User Interface)
SGI O2 R5000
200 MHz CPU
128 MB RAM
4 GB Hard Disk
CD-ROM
17" Monitor

Update Rate: 50 Hz/60 Hz

No. of Polygons: 10,000K-70,000K (Postproduction mode can run more)

Modelers: Alias; Softimage; Softimage 3-D; Alias Wavefront Power Animator; Alias Wavefront Maya; 3-Dstudio MAX; Lightscape; Hoodiny; MultiGen OpenFlight format; Alias Wavefront OBJ format; AutoCAD DXF format; Inventor format; VRML format

Keyers: Analog and Digital

Switchers: Analog and Digital

Video Standards: PAL/NTSC/16:9; SECAM; HDTV

Video Inputs: two full resolutions

Tracking Systems:
Thoma Tracking systems
Vinten TSM
Radamec
BBC's FreeD
Mark Roberts Milo
Walk Finder
Xync, X-Pecto

Hokeye
Crane
Dolly
PVI and others

Interface to ext. Devices:
Lighting Computer
VTR
DDR
DVE
Router
Keyer
Phone Control
Generic Plug-in
Audio Mixer
Character Generator
Motion Capture

Pica Virtual Billboard Product Description:
RT-SET's Pica is a new virtual billboard product for use in television and production studios. Pica enables the user to hold and move a simple board on
which live video, pictures or 3-D graphics images can appear. All the images
seen on the billboard change in the correct perspective, according to camera
movements or movements of the anchor holding the billboard, in real-time.

  Pica consists of a chroma-key blue or green board that is replaced by the
video or picture inserted. It is easy to use and to integrate into any standard or
virtual production studio. Pica is utilized in a variety of ways—it displays statistics, weather, news clips, animations, educational items and many more. The
user has complete control over the location of the board at all times, making it
easier than ever to present information to viewers, live on-air, in the clearest
and easiest manner.

❖ To be used in standard or virtual studio.

❖ Can work with any video standard.

❖ The best way to present results, statistics, animation.

Pica Features:

❖ Full video resolution appears on the billboard at all times.

❖ Standard and Blue Screen Studios compatible.

❖ Billboard can be rotated in any way desired—in all axes.

❖ Simple setup procedure, with one friendly user interface screen.

❖ No operator required.

❖ No restrictions on the camera movements.

❖ Video window can appear in front of or behind the talent.

❖ No dedicated hardware is needed.

System Specifications

Pica Graphics Computer:
SGI O2 R5000
200 MHz CPU
192 MB RAM
4 GB Hard Disk
CD-ROM
17" Monitor

Update Rate: 50 Hz/60 Hz

Keyers: Analog and Digital

Switchers: Analog and Digital

Standards: PAL/NTSC, SECAM

Discreet

Frost* data

Frost* is a resolution-independent 3-D graphics system for broadcast production. With real-time external control capabilities, the system is ideal for everyday news, financial, and sports graphics, or for complex graphic animations that typically require multiple character generators, digital disk recorders, DVE channels, and video sources. It is reliable and easy to learn and to use.

Frost* renders 3-D imagery and text in real-time, based on cues from external sources such as touch-screens, newswires, sports statistics databases, and stock quote services. Frost* makes developing and maintaining a station identity cost effective. Frost* graphics templates can be quickly updated and reused. Frost* has an upgrade path to graphics production at HDTV resolution, and to an all-digital virtual production studio, where broadcast graphics and live-action shots can be immersed in photorealistic 3-D sets.

Features

3-D Authoring Environment

❖ Integrated set of 3-D authoring tools for broadcast graphics design

❖ Ability to quickly create and edit templates

❖ Apply 2-D stills or motion video onto 3-D objects without external DVE

❖ Interface to light* radiosity renderer to create photorealistic sets

❖ Object import tools (supported formats include 3DS, OBJ, FLT, DXF, IV, AND, VRML)

❖ Hierarchical view of the scene database for grouping/parenting/inheritance/drag and drop

❖ Open and edit multiple scenes simultaneously

❖ Access most commonly used functions via hotkeys

❖ Unlimited number of undo levels

❖ Four viewpoint 3-D editor with direct manipulation

❖ Project management

❖ Integrated set of tools for project management

❖ User-friendly interface reduces the need for UNIX commands

❖ Graphics templates can be easily retrieved and archived

Object Properties Editor

❖ Built-in 2-D and 3-D object primitives

❖ Full control over an object's level-of-detail (tesselation)

❖ All object properties can be animated

❖ Up to eight light sources (local, infinite, spotlight) with animations

❖ Software anti-aliasing (for use when hardware anti-aliasing is unavailable)

Links

❖ Ideal for workgroup environment; simultaneous use by multiple users in multiple 3-D graphic scenes

❖ Use reference links to lock and unlock the attributes of graphic elements, such as logos

Transformation Editor

❖ Six degrees-of-freedom (DOF) for precise positioning of objects

❖ Direct manipulation of objects in rendering windows

Motion Path Animation

❖ Create and manipulate motion paths interactively in 3-D space using control points and tangents

❖ Animate individual objects along a path, with full control over orientation and velocity

Animation Editor

❖ Unlimited keyframe animation on any 3-D element with manual and auto-keyframing

❖ Direct curve editing on animation channels

❖ Nonlinear editing of independent animation timelines

❖ Animation groups and external control allow operators to make changes from a remote PC

Text

❖ Support for Adobe Type 1 PostScripts, financial, and Asian (CID) fonts (dual-byte)

❖ Visual and full control over font, size, position, and kerning

❖ Real-time beveled 3-D text

❖ Manipulate material and texture on front, back, and side of each typeface

- ❖ Support for accented and special characters
- ❖ Automated text entry from file or remote PC (requires Producer On-Air Suite)
- ❖ The following languages are supported: ASCII, ISO 8859-1: English, French, German, Spanish, Catalan, Basque, Portuguese, Italian, Albanian, Dutch, Danish, Swedish, Norwegian, Finnish, Icelandic, Irish; ISO 8859-2: Czech, Hungarian, Polish, Romanian, Croatian, Slovak, Slovenian, Serbian; ISO 8859-5: Cyrillic (Russian, Bulgarian, Byelorussian, and Serbian); ISO 8859-7: Greek; ISO 8859-9: Turkish; KOI8R: Cyrillic (Russian); EUC/Hankaku/JIS/RKSJ: Japanese; Big-5(PC): Traditional Chinese; GB: Simplified Chinese; Wansung/KSC5601/Johab: Hangul (Korean)

Material and Texture Editors

- ❖ Texture mapping options: direct, linear, and reflection
- ❖ Textures can be positioned, rotated and scaled interactively with color and transparency control
- ❖ Animate texture mapping coordinates to create moving backgrounds images without additional video sources and keyers
- ❖ Asynchronous texture loading of background images without affecting on-air performance
- ❖ MIP mapping filtering to reduce minification artifacts
- ❖ Visual browser to provide quick and easy access to texture files, materials, and video clips
- ❖ Still texture formats: RGB, RGBA, TIFF, BW, and JPEG

Animated Texture Formats:

DIVO input, ITU-R 601 video + key
Discreet Storage RGB 4:4:4
AVI, MPEG, QuickTime, and SGI Movie

Production Environment

- ❖ High-performance resolution independent renderer
- ❖ Multiprocess architecture for consistent, real-time frame rate management
- ❖ Real-time performance statistics
- ❖ Load multiple 3-D graphics or scenes simultaneously

❖ Transition easily between virtual camera view points (up to 8)

❖ Control from remote PC operator console

❖ Control Leitch 16 x16 Xplus digital video routers for video source input selection

Options

❖ light* for Windows NT or 95 to create photorealistic sets

❖ Discreet Storage and Discreet Networking Utility

❖ Producer On-Air Suite (external control software for Windows NT/95)

❖ Discreet Background I/O Utility for framestore management and image input

Video and Audio I/ O

❖ 525/625 line ITU-R-601 video in and out with key

❖ SGI audio for sound effects and clip playback (AIFF, MIDI, WAV)

❖ Support for 16:9 HDTV formats

Automated Graphics Finishing

❖ Modify any aspect of a scene from another computer via TCP/IP networking

❖ Update 3-D data-driven graphics manually or automatically from external source

❖ Trigger animations on demand Trigger audio clip playback and external devices such as DDRs and VTRs

❖ Query frost* for information about the scene or any object in the scene

❖ Control frost* during rehearsals and throughout the entire production process

Virtual Studio Module

❖ Camera tracking and studio registration tools, seamlessly integrating real and virtual elements

❖ Transform scenes into immersive 3-D scenes for mixed computer graphics and live-action production

❖ Scene registration process accurately matches virtual to real stage with little effort

❖ Visualize blue screen, blue objects, camera positions, orientations, and incoming raw data

❖ Camera viewpoints can track up to 6 degrees of freedom (pan/tilt/roll/x/y/z) and lens parameters (zoom/focus)

sparks*

❖ sparks* developer's program available to third party developers

❖ Virtual camera API specification available to developers of camera tracking systems

Related Terms and Acronyms

The explanations given here relate only to meanings relevant to virtual studio and TV. Other meanings of terms are ignored.

2-D—Two dimensional, flat.

3-D—Three dimensions—length, width, and depth.

A/D—Analog to Digital conversion. Conversion of an analog signal such as composite video to a digital signal such as SDI.

Analog—The opposite of digital. A signal that can have an infinite number of levels. The levels in analog signals usually represent values of variants such as audio level in sound signals and luminance in video.

Background—In classical television, the actual physical set; in virtual studio sets—a still or live picture placed behind the image of a subject or performers.

Bleeding color—a color that is usually highly saturated and spills beyond its defined limits.

Blue box—A studio or space where the floor and walls are painted blue and equipped with appropriate lighting to enable the creation of chroma-key effects.

Blue screen—A blue background such as a large blue cloth used for chroma-key effects in a TV or film studio.

CCTV—Closed Circuit Television. Television signals carried by cables to a limited number of users.

CD—Compact Disk. A 5.25" optical disk with a 650 MB capacity used to store audio and data.

Chroma-Key—A process used in TV to replace the background of an object or performer in the studio. The blue color (or any other color) is replaced by information from another source such as a still picture, live video or graphics.

Chroma-Keyer—An electronic device that replaces one defined color in a video signal with another video signal.

Component—Video picture information carried by three separate signals, Y, B-Y, R-Y. This was an improvement of the composite system before the age of digital hardware.

Composite—An analog video signal that includes all components of the picture such as luminance, chrominance, synchronization pulses and also test signals (VITC), time code and teletext.

Compression—Techniques used to reduce the size of computer files and the bandwidth of electronic signals.

CPU—Central Processing Unit. The heart of computers executing most of the calculations and control functions.

Crane—A long mechanical arm that can carry a camera high in the air. Used to perform camera movements not possible with a tripod or a pedestal.

Cyclorama—A large curtain that usually surrounds the walls of TV studios. The cyclorama comes in different colors, normally blue is used for chroma-key effects, sometimes green.

D/A—Digital to Analog conversion. A device that converts digital signals such as SDI to an analog signal such as composite video.

DBS—Direct Broadcast Satellite. A transmission system where a satellite or set of satellites is used to distribute large numbers of television channels.

Defocus—A state in which a picture is not focused, usually to obtain a certain visual effect. A defocused background creates good depth feeling if a figure in the foreground is focused.

Delay line—A device used to prolong the time taken for an electronic signal to get from one point to another by a specific amount of time.

Digital—The opposite of analog, a signal that is composed of two levels only representing zeros and ones. Computers and modern communications devices use digital signals.

Dissolve—A "soft" transition between pictures—one fades out while the other appears gradually.

Dolly—A camera support on wheels that is used to get camera shots in motion, also a name of camera movement where the camera moves in parallel to action.

Ethernet—A very common local area network transport protocol.

Fill—The information input in a chroma-key process instead of blue or other signal taken out.

Floor manager—The person in charge of the activity in the studio during production.

Foreground—The space in front of the image of a subject or performer in the studio, or picture.

Garbage matte—A process used to hide parts of an image such as the ceiling in a TV studio or other parts that are not covered with cyclorama or properly lit.

GIF—Graphic Interchange Format. A common format for graphic files.

Graphic engine—Hardware, software or both that are used to perform operations (rendering) on graphic files.

HDTV—High Definition Television. Television signals with a high amount of detail—five times as much as in standard definition TV. The number of picture lines in the American system is 1,125 and the frame rate is 60.

Infrared—Radiation with a frequency close to, but lower than, visible light, therefore invisible to the human eye. Some specially adapted cameras can operate in such wavelengths.

ITU-R 601—An international standard that defines the structure of component digital video. This is the most common digital video signal in TV today.

JPEG—Joint Photographic Experts Group. A standard of data compression used in graphics and video. Compression rates can range between 5 and 100, depending on various parameters.

Keying—A process used to remove parts of a picture and insert others instead. Removal is made according to a predefined attribute such as luminance or hue.

Key signal—A signal that defines the exact parts in a picture to be replaced by others. Also known as Alfa.

LED—Light Emitting Diode. An small electronic component that emits light in an efficient way.

Linux—A free, open code operating system for PCs, based on UNIX.

Live—A program or event transmitted to viewers in real time.

Luminance key—A keying process made according to the luminance of a picture. The brightest or darkest parts are replaced by other picture information.

Motion control—The control of the movement of motorized camera pan and tilt heads and/or pedestals by electronic means. This allows accurate repetition of movement and retrieval accurate motion information.

Motion tracking—Retrieval of motion data from a camera or camera support system while it moves and changes position and orientation.

MPEG—Motion Pictures Expert Group. A set of standards for compression of digital audio and video signals set up by industry experts. The MPEG compression rate changes according to the complexity of the picture content. Several levels are defined, to support different kings of signals and qualities.

NTSC—National Television Systems Committee. A transmission standard used in North America, some parts of South America and Japan.

O.B. van—Outside Broadcast Van. A vehicle equipped with cameras and other TV equipment that allows transmission of events and programs from the field.

On-air—A program, which is currently being transmitted to viewers.

PAL—Phase Alternating Lines. An analog transmission system used in most of the world except North America and Japan, and those regions using the French SECAM system. (*See* **SECAM.**)

Pan—A horizontal camera movement.

Pattern recognition—In virtual studio system a method of retrieving camera movement information from the video signal it produces. Bar codes or a grid identifiable to the system computer must be positioned in the field of view of the camera objects.

Photo-realistic—Graphics that appear to be a photographic representation of something or place from real life.

Pixel—Picture cell. The smallest element of which a picture is made up.

Polygon—In 3-D graphics all objects are made of polygons which are triangles combined together to form more complex objects.

Postproduction—All operations performed after a shooting and recording of a program or event.

Preproduction—The preparation stages before a program is taped or aired from the studio.

Prerendered—In a virtual studio system, graphic material rendered in the pre-production stage. Usually in cases where the main graphic engine cannot render the graphic files live according to camera motion. This requires that cameras perform predefined motion during production.

Preview—In a TV studio control room a monitor that shows the next source to be taken to air. Also used to adjust visual effects such as key and wipe before being taken on-air.

Real time—Computation that is fast enough not to delay or slow the process involved. In virtual studio systems the rendering of virtual set according to camera movement has to be performed at field rate, 60 times per second.

Rendering—Processing of changes in graphic files.

Resolution—The amount of detail in a picture of any kind, usually measured in pixels or TV lines.

RGB—A video format in which picture information is provided separately in three channels of red, green and blue information.

RS-232—A serial protocol for data transfer between computers. Uses two twisted pairs and is usually limited in range to less than 100 feet.

RS-422—A serial protocol for data transfer between computers for ranges of up to 1,000 feet. Uses two twisted pairs and is very common in TV installations.

Scenery—A background used in TV studios to create a real or imaginary environment. Usually made of materials such as plywood, metal, and cardboard, and painted.

SDI—Serial Digital Interface. A standard for digital component video. Complies with ITU-R 601.

SECAM—Sequential Colour Avec Memoire. Developed by France and used by certain countries in Europe and North Africa.

Set—Scenery.

Steadicam—Trade name for a device used to carry a camera and shoot while walking or running which greatly reduces body movement and vibration that are transferred to the camera.

TIF—A standard graphics file format used for bitmap images.

Tilt—Vertical camera movement, up and down on an axis that goes through the camera center or located under the center of the camera.

UNIX—An operating system, which utilizes advanced multitasking and multiuser capabilities. Used by SGI in O2 and Onyx computers.

VCR—Videocassette Recorder. Used in television to record and play back audio and video signals.

Virtual—Exists only in a computer.

Virtual set—A scenery or background which is not real and is composed of a 2-D or 3-D graphic artwork.

Virtual studio—A non-real environment created in computers to replace the ordinary studio and scenery environment.

Zoom—Change in focal length of a TV camera lens that results in a smooth magnification or reduction of the output image. Zoom is a camera movement frequently used during shooting of video segments.

Virtual Studio Users

The following list is composed partially of names of customers supplied by the various manufacturers as well as users discovered by researching trade publications

3DV, Inc. USA

ABC News, USA

AIT, Nigeria

America 2, Argentina

America TV (Canal 4), Peru

Antena 3, Spain

Asia Business News, Singapore

Asia Television Ltd. (ATV), Hong
   Kong

Atlantic Video, USA

ATV, Hong Kong

ATV, Turkey

AV Technology, Hong Kong

Bablsberg Fx Center, Germany

BBC, England

BBC Sports, UK

BBC TV Centre, UK

BBC VR Facility, UK

Beijing TV (BTV), China

Bloomberg, USA

Blue Space Media Germany,

B-SKY-B, UK

BTL, China

BTV, China

Canal 12, Uruguay

Canal 13 TV, Paraguay

Canal 4 M. Carlo, Uruguay

Canal 4 TV, Paraguay

Capriccioso, Japan

Caracol TRR, (RCN) Columbia

CBC TV, USA

CBS 2, USA

CCTV, China

Channel 11, Thailand

China Central Television (CCTV),
China

Color Cassettes, Mexico

CVM, Jamaica

Cyber Studio, Hungary

Derwen, UK

Deutches Sportsfernsehen, Germany

Digital Production Resources, USA

Discovery Channel, USA

DR, Denmark

Dubai Business Channel, UAE

Emirates Broadcasting Corp, UAE

Endemol/NOB, Holland

ESPN, USA

European Parliament, France

Eurosport, France

Exa International, Japan

Florida News Channel, USA

For A Sakura R&D, Japan

Frenter Communications / Tele
  Monte Carlo, Italy

Gamavision, Ecuador

Gaung Zhou Cable TV, China

General Motors, USA

Gestmusic Endemol, Spain

Global Broadcasting Co. Taiwan

Grupo Artec y Technologia S.A.,
  Mexico

Hadassah College, Israel

IBA, Israel

Infobyte, Italy

Inter, Ukrain

ISL TV, UK

ITN—Channel 4 News, UK

ITN News, UK

ITN, UK

ITV, UK

KBS, Korea

KKYK, USA

The Learning Channel, USA

Liga D.I., Georgia

LRP Digital, USA

Madison Square Garden Network,
  USA

MAV srl, Italy

MBC, Korea

Ministry of Posts and
  Telecommunications, Japan

Mirage Digital LLC, USA

Molinare, UK

MTV, Hungary

Multimedia Akademie Bayren,
  Germany

NDR, Germany

Nitrofilm Medienproduktion,
  Germany

NRK, Norway

NTL Langley, UK

NTT Human Interface Lab, Japan

NTT Learning Systems, Japan

NTV, Russia

ONTV, Canada

Option Facilities, Belgum

ORAD

ORF, Austria

Pacific Title Mirage, USA

PanAmericana TV (Canal 5), Peru

Polsat, Poland

Post Effects, USA

The Production Group, USA

ProSyLab, Egypt

Pyramid, UK

RAI, Italy

RTE, Ireland

RTP, Portugal

RTV, Yugoslavia

Rugo Kommunikation, Germany

SBP, Italy

SBS, Australia

SBT Channel 4, Brazil

Seven Network, Australia

Shahar, Kazakhstan

Shanghai TV, China

Show TV, Turkey

SIC, Portugal

Skai, Greece

SMA Video, USA

South African Rugby Union, South
    Africa

Sport TV, Hungary

Sport TV, Venezuela

Sports Channel, Israel

Sunshine Networks, USA

Supersport (filmnet), Greece

SZM, Germany

SZM Studios, Germany

Taiwan Tainan National College of
    the Arts, Taiwan

TeleCinco, Spain

Tele-Europe, France

Telefe, Argentina

Televisa S.A. de C.V., Mexico

Televisa, Mexico

Television Nacional de Chile (TVN),
    Chile

TF1, France

Tivionica, Russia

Torneos, Argentina

TSN, Canada

TU Ilmenau, Germany

TV2, Norway

TV 4, Sweden

TV Asahi, Japan

TV Azteca, Mexico

TV Globo, Brazil

TV Record, Brazil

TVBS, Taiwan

TVF Studio, Germany

TVI Network, India

TVN, Chile

TVNZ, New Zealand

UCTV, Chile

Ultimate Video, Holland

Venevision, Venezuela

Video Cairo, Egypt

Videocation, Germany

Videoimage, France

WDR, Germany

Wige Data, Germany

WSI, UK

Index